JUSTICE
WHILE
BLACK

JUSTICE
WHILE
BLACK

**Helping African-American Families
Navigate and Survive
the Criminal Justice System**

Robbin Shipp, Esq. AND Nick Chiles

BOLDEN

AN AGATE IMPRINT

CHICAGO

Printed in the United States of America

Library of Congress Cataloging-in-Publication Data

Shipp, Robbin, author.
 Justice while black : helping African-American families navigate and survive the criminal justice system / Robbin Shipp, Nick Chiles.
      pages cm
 Summary: "Advice for African-American families about dealing with specific legal circumstances such as avoiding arrest, being in custody, going through a trial, the and parole process"--Provided by publisher.
  ISBN-13: 978-1-932841-90-9 (paperback)
  ISBN-10: 1-932841-90-3 (paperback)
  ISBN-13: 978-1-57284-741-5 (ebook)
 1. African Americans--Legal status, laws, etc.--United States. 2. African Americans--Civil rights. 3. Criminal justice, Administration of--United States. 4. Discrimination in criminal justice administration--United States. 5. Discrimination in law enforcement--United States. 6. Race discrimination--Law and legislation--United States. I. Chiles, Nick, author. II. Title.
  KF4757.S55 2014
  345.730089'96073--dc23
                                        2014027950

10 9 8 7 6 5 4 3 2 1

Bolden is an imprint of Agate Publishing. Agate books are available in bulk at discount prices. For more information, go to agatepublishing.com.

To my parents, Robert and Carrie Shipp, without whom I would not be, I love you both dearly. To my daughter, Alex, of whom I am very proud. And to all of the young men in my life who inspired me to want to write this. I hope your future is made brighter by this book's existence.
—ROBBIN

To my son Mazi, my daughters Mari and Lila, my nephews Miles and Cole, and all the talented and capable young men and women I've encountered on my journeys over the years, every day when I awake I recommit myself to fighting for a world that looks at you and sees sweetness and joy.
—NICK

Table of Contents

Foreword

THIS BOOK IS the culmination of my life's work as a criminal defense attorney in the state of Georgia. During my more than eighteen-year career, I have been privileged to represent many young, African-American men charged with crimes against the citizens of the state. Often, I would enter their lives while they were enduring tremendous stress and anguish, yet almost to a one, these young men were respectful, engaging, and at times humorous when discussing the circumstances that put them behind bars.

Three years in the making, this book is intended as a guide to help anyone ensnared in the criminal justice system. Unfortunately, in this nation, that typically means African-American males.

After we shelved the original outline for two years, this book was reborn after the verdict in the Trayvon Martin murder trial. Not since my father's death have I cried as much as I did when the Zimmerman verdict was read. I cried because, as Fannie

Lou Hamer said, "I was sick and tired of being sick and tired." I cried over this nation's propensity to be okay with the mass incarceration and death of hundreds of thousands of African-American men.

Do African-American men commit crimes? Yes, they do. But white men do as well. It's the disproportion in punishment that takes your breath away. Of the 2.3 million Americans in prison, more than 840,000 are black males. More than a third, in a country where only about 12 percent of the population is African American. Of the 200,000 females in prison, 65,000 are black females. Something is wrong here.

When it comes to murder, we don't see white men and women being gunned down under the guise of "standing your ground." That distinction seems reserved for African Americans.

Black males and police forces have been warring combatants since this nation's founding, when wealthy planters hired slave patrols to capture escaped slaves and to keep the white community safe from dangerous brown bodies.

The tactics have been modernized, but the impact is still devastating—we are witnessing an epic criminalization of the African-American community at levels never before seen in the history of global civilizations. Lawyer and author Michelle Alexander calls it a "new Jim Crow," which is creating a new caste system that is destroying the fabric of the African-American community.

But it's one thing to bemoan the numbers, another thing entirely to do something about them. So we wrote this book in hopes of providing education and guidance for African-American men, and their families, to avoid the greedy jaws of the prison-industrial complex. Should they find themselves caught in its jaws, we try to offer ways they can minimize its negative impact on their lives.

This book isn't intended as a substitution for effective counsel, or as a magic spell to get you out of legal trouble. But hopefully the lessons, stories, and advice on these pages will give you a clear idea of how to minimize your difficulties and distress at each step in the legal process.

Stay safe.

Robbin Shipp, Esq.

Chapter 1: Officer Friendly Isn't Your Friend

Everything You Need to Know about Racial Profiling

IN ARIZONA, it's Hispanics.

In the South, it's African Americans.

In California, it's Hispanics and African Americans.

In New York City, it's everybody with brown skin—Arabs, African Americans, Hispanics.

Targets. All.

Victims.

For no reason other than the color of their skin. The texture of their hair. The language they speak. The country where they were born.

We have become a nation where many police forces have resorted to quick and easy racial identifiers to determine who is suspect, who is criminal, who should be locked up. In recent years this practice has come to be known as "racial profiling," but for groups like African Americans it has long been a dispiriting, inescapable part of our existence. For African Americans, it can be called, simply, "life."

Though the US Constitution and US courts prohibit racial profiling, the practice is still prevalent across the nation. Stopping it appears to be as tricky as removing hate from the human heart. Hardly a week goes by without another alarming media report chronicling another outrageous case of a racist cop, an overly aggressive retail store clerk, or an out-of-control school security officer singling out a person of color for some outrageously heinous act. These stories race across the Internet as fleet as a Beyoncé–Jay Z rumor, spreading outrage and consternation in their wake.

Freedom from official tyranny, from an overzealous state, is one of those rights that most Americans take for granted. We step out of our front doors expecting a form of invisibility from law enforcement—*don't call us, we'll call you.* Until we summon them, we don't expect much interaction with the police.

But for black men under 40, that expectation of invisibility is just a fantasy. Sixty years after Ralph Ellison published his aching cry against the black man's irrelevancy and powerlessness in *Invisible Man*, the black man ironically is now all too visible in the eyes of American law enforcement. From the West Coast to the East, from the frigid North to the sweltering South, black boys and young black men move through their days enveloped in a cloak of suspicion. When many of us consider the stunning statistics concerning black boys and the criminal justice system, our response tracks along the lines of "Well, if they didn't commit any crimes, they wouldn't be going to jail."

But that thinking misses the cold efficiency of the prison-industrial complex, which requires a steady supply of bodies—suspects, defendants, inmates, ex-cons on probation—to sustain itself. In certain neighborhoods in certain cities of this nation, it seems nearly impossible for a black boy to make it to manhood without being sucked into the system. In Washington, DC, an estimated three out of four young black men—and nearly all of those from the poorest neighborhoods—can expect to serve time in prison. In some of our major cities, as many as 80 percent of young black males have criminal records.

In 2003, the Bureau of Justice Statistics released a report that was received like a nuclear bomb in many quarters: One in every three young black men in the US could expect to be incarcerated at some point in his life.

And though educators and activists in many communities report that the circumstances facing black females in this country have grown increasingly precarious, black males are much more likely to wind up in prison. While the US prison population in 2009 was 39.4 percent black, that number consisted of 841,000 black males and 64,800 black females (out of a total prison population of 2,096,300 males and 201,200 females), according to the US Bureau of Justice Statistics. Currently there are thirteen black males in prison for every black female.

Racial profiling takes many sinister forms in the US, stimulated by a toxic mix of stereotyping, bias, and laziness. One of the most far-reaching is expressed in the sentencing disparities evident in many areas of the criminal justice system, most notably in drug cases.

Though blacks and whites use marijuana in roughly the same proportions, a report by the ACLU found that in 2010 blacks were approximately 4 times more likely than whites to be arrested for marijuana possession—a "crime" that isn't even a crime any more in parts of the country that have legalized marijuana.

In Washington, DC, blacks were an astounding eight times more likely than whites to be arrested for marijuana possession.

I've seen these disparities firsthand in my law practice, over and over again. When I got out of law school, I tried to approach the law with the mindset of race neutrality, wanting to believe that, indeed, the law is colorblind. But over time, I had to let go of that delusion, confronted with some very harsh realities.

While I was handling a seemingly endless stream of cases involving young black males being sent to prison for simple drug possession, I saw that the judicial system often had different ideas about how to handle cases involving white male defendants. I saw a white man in a rural Georgia county arrested for drug manufacturing—he was growing pot in his house—receive a sentence of just three to five years on probation. That was it. For a manufacturer, arrested with the drugs and the manufacturing equipment in his house.

The case of this white manufacturer was fresh in my mind when the court appointed me to represent a young black male who had been arrested for selling crack cocaine. It involved a simple one-hit sale of a small quantity of the drug. And I was going before the same judge who earlier gave the white manufacturer a probated sentence. The prosecutor wanted my client to go to prison, but I had another resolution in mind. I told the court about the extraordinary circumstances that accompanied his drug sale—his brother had just been killed saving the life of an elderly lady suffering from dementia who had wandered into the street. Still grappling with grief, he went out and sold crack. I admitted to the judge that this wasn't the best way to handle grief, but he was wracked with considerable pain.

The judge sentenced my client to probation and a stay at a diversion center. The public defenders in the courtroom were stunned—they told me it was the best plea deal they'd ever seen. They said that this kind of plea was virtually unheard of in that county, where prison was seen as mandatory if you pled guilty to a drug sale. No exceptions. Before the judge announced the sentence, in my head I was grappling with the question of whether to bring up the case of the white manufacturer if the judge announced that he was sending my client to prison. Fortunately, the judge did what I had hoped. I would like to think that the judge modified his standard sentencing because of the extraordinary distress the defendant was enduring, but as I look back now, I suspect that the judge knew that I was aware of the sentence he gave to the white manufacturer. I hope he knew he would have to come correct, likely thinking something along the lines of, *Oh no, this crazy black woman attorney is going to raise holy hell.*

These drug possession cases, which often begin with some type of racial profiling practiced by the police, are now the lifeblood—or the cancer, depending on where you sit—of the American criminal justice system. According to the FBI's annual Crime in the US report, of the 12.2 million arrests in the US in 2012, only property crime (1.64 million) was more common than drug possession (1.55 million). In recent years, drug possession has often meant just marijuana possession—nearly half of the drug possession arrests in the FBI report were for marijuana.

The brutal "War on Drugs" that has raged in this country since the 1980s—Michelle Alexander brilliantly revealed in *The New Jim Crow: Mass Incarceration in the Age of Colorblindedness* that the war was waged to create a steady supply of defendants for the prison-industrial complex—initially focused largely on the explosion of crack in poor communities of color. But as the crack epidemic waned in the late 1980s, law enforcement agencies shifted to the easiest of targets: marijuana.

In 2010, according to the ACLU, more than 20,000 people were incarcerated simply for possessing marijuana. The 889,133 marijuana arrests in 2010—a tally that comes out to one arrest every 37 seconds—was 300,000 more than arrests for all violent crimes combined.

Imagine how different black communities would look if law enforcement directed its resources away from marijuana possession arrests and concentrated on crimes of greater import to society. Imagine how much better the lives of a generation of black males—

and the lives of their families and children—would have been if they had been free to explore their dreams and utilize their talents, and rather than being incarcerated, they had instead received counseling and treatment. Imagine how much better off our entire nation would be if those black males had been free to do that.

Since the 1970s, criminal defendants in Georgia had access to a sentence review panel to which they could appeal sentences that might be overly harsh. The panel, which was made up of three state judges, would consider the facts of the case and sometimes reduce sentences—though it only happened in about 3 percent of the approximately 1,000 cases sent to the panel every year. This provided an essential check and balance to a system that in many cases saw huge disparities in sentences imposed by judges throughout Georgia's judicial circuits. At least it did until 2007, when it was abolished.

Other states, such as Maryland, Montana, and Maine, still have sentencing review panels similar to those that used to operate in Georgia—and I should point out that a few of those panels have been under attack in recent years.

I don't think I'm exaggerating in saying that the review panel in Georgia was despised by most prosecutors, sheriffs, and other law enforcement entities. But in a state like Georgia, where rural authorities could exploit their isolation and autonomy, often to the detriment of African-American defendants, it was an important final protection against prosecutorial and judicial overzealousness and bias.

But finally, after years of much fuming in some quarters about the existence of the panels, one judge had had too much. When the review panel seriously reduced the sentence of a black man she had slapped with a harsh sentence—a man whose record had been fairly clean until the offense in question—this judge, after first attempting to stop the Department of Corrections from enacting the panel's decision (reduction of the defendant's sentence), held a hearing on a motion of the prosecutor and declared that the sentence review panel was unconstitutional. In a 2003 opinion, the Georgia Supreme Court disagreed with that decision, but did so due to that judge lacking the subject matter jurisdiction to make that decision. This ruling set up a lobbying effort by the same judge for the Georgia legislature to eliminate the sentence review panel. While I was serving in the Georgia state legislature as a state representative (from 2007 to 2009), during the 2007 legislative session the Republican-controlled body—my colleagues on the other side of the aisle—passed a bill that abolished the sentence review panel. For me, this was yet another painful reminder of the extent to which state legislatures in the US dictate the rules by which we live our lives—usually without most Americans ever realizing it. For African Americans, these state legislatures are puppet masters that secretly control and circumscribe our lives. Like the Wizard of Oz, they hide behind a curtain of anonymity—a curtain created by the indifference of a public that rarely pays attention to the actions of the legislatures and a media that doesn't effectively cover them.

In recent years, Georgia has begun to funnel large amounts of state funding into treatment programs for methamphetamine addicts. If you aren't aware, meth has become the drug of choice for suburban and rural white kids. In creating diversion and treatment programs, the state can offer an alternative to sending these kids to prison. As I have shown, the prisons are reserved for a different (darker) population.

The most common form of racial profiling occurs when a police officer pulls over one or a group of young black males in an automobile. The vehicle stop is the reveille, the bugle call that initiates the entire legal drama that many of us have come to describe as "driving while black."

It is important to recognize that in the minds of the police, everything is about justifying the stop. As long as they have a justification, they can legally stop anyone they want. That means much of an officer's behavior can be understood by considering his primary motivation during every stop he makes: finding the justification to make the stop rise to the legal definition of "reasonable." If the case makes it to court—or at least comes to the attention of a defense attorney—this is where much of that attorney's efforts will focus.

"Officer, why did you stop this young man?"

Though it may be obvious to some, I need to point out here that police officers are not always white. The imperative to slap handcuffs on as many wrists as possible isn't limited to white cops. There have been many cases across the country, including in states like Florida and Texas, where black officers were accused of racial profiling. And when I say police officer, I'm really talking about the patrolling forces in counties and municipalities with the legal authority to make arrests. While this usually means a police department in an urban setting, it could also mean sheriff's departments in rural or suburban settings. In my experience, police officers tend to share a mindset: Control of the streets is an epic battle of *us* (law enforcement) versus *them* (the rest of society).

These police stops can begin with an officer responding to a call after a specific type of incident: someone's home was broken into, somebody's vehicle was carjacked, somewhere nearby there's been an armed robbery. The nature of the crime will dictate how many officers respond—something violent will bring a larger swarm. Invariably, a victim will have given a description. And this is where things get dicey for young black males. The description is often so general as to be almost useless. So we have officers cruising around, looking for a vehicle that fits the description of the vehicle used in the crime, if there was a vehicle used, and looking for individuals who fit the description of the individuals who committed the offense.

As a defense attorney, I know that witness identification is a precarious business. Usually victims are so shaken up by the incident that they are only able to give very general descriptions: things like "black male, white T-shirt, dreadlocks" or "black male, gray hoodie, bald head." The victim might have just had a gun pointed in her face, with a strange, scary man yelling at her to do something she is quite disinclined to do: Empty out the cash register! Open up the safe! Load all those blue jeans on the shelves into these bags! In cases of sexual assault, just hours or minutes earlier, he might have forced himself inside of her while holding a gun to her head. In these incredibly traumatizing circumstances, with so many wild and fearful thoughts racing through her mind, it is very hard to formulate an accurate, precise description of an assailant unless he has an unusual identifying characteristic, such as a scar on his face or a crazy hairstyle.

A growing body of research has highlighted the likelihood of inaccuracies in eyewitness identifications. The Innocence Project estimates that eyewitness misidentification plays a role in nearly 75 percent of convictions overturned through DNA testing, making it the single greatest cause of wrongful convictions in the nation. When researchers conduct controlled experiments to test the accuracy of eyewitness identifications, they have found that eyewitnesses incorrectly identify strangers at about the same rate as they identify them correctly. That's a horrible truth, especially considering how compelling and powerful eyewitness testimony is to judges and juries and how frequently it is used to send defendants to prison for a long time.

Compounding the problem significantly is the added unreliability of cross-racial eyewitness identification. People are much more likely to misidentify a stranger of another race. And most appallingly for black males, white people appear to have an especially hard time identifying African Americans, according to researchers.

Despite all of these disturbing considerations, eyewitness identification remains the fuel that powers most law enforcement investigations and prosecutions, often to the detriment of black male defendants. So when a crime is committed and a search commences, the description the police are often working with is something like "black male, 5-10, short cropped hair, dark skinned in complexion, age 27–33."

Do you know how many black men will fit that description? It could fit the guy in blue jeans and a white T-shirt, with a silver-colored watch and an earring in his left ear, hurriedly walking down the street because he's late for the bus. That hurried gait might lead to a truly awful day for him. It could fit the guy who just walked out of the barbershop 10 minutes earlier after getting a shape-up on his bushy Afro. But unfortunately for him, the barbershop happens to be in the same general vicinity where the crime occurred. So with all of these police officers responding to the call, swarming the area, they're inevitably going to grab this guy as he's trying to get into his car.

The description might also fit the guy who's rushing to pick up his kid from school at 3 p.m., driving a little too fast down the street in his Dodge Charger—a popular car with African-American young men. In an instant, he's swept into the clutches of the police—leaving his poor child waiting for a loooong time. The squad car pulls him over. The cop might later say that he looked nervous or agitated or overly upset—as if any black man is going to be nonchalant when an officer is approaching him for an unknown reason. The officer is going to tell him to get out of the car. If the victim of the crime is able, the police might do a "show-up"—holding the potential suspect until another squad car drives the victim to the scene to identify him. Or they may forgo all of that and just arrest him on suspicion of having committed the crime in question.

The tragic death of teenager Kendrec McDade in Pasadena shows how precarious and potentially fatal are the words the police hear from the crime victim. When Oscar Carrillo called 911 to report that his computer had been stolen, Carrillo lied and told the dispatcher that he had been robbed at gunpoint—he thought this would yield a quicker police response. Security video later showed a young man taking a computer from Carrillo's car. McDade is seen on the video standing near the rear of the car.

But after they got the call, Officers Jeffrey prison and Matthew Griffin responded with the belief that they were looking for an armed assailant. When they spotted nineteen-year-old McDade running down the street, they said they saw his right hand at his waist. So as Officer Griffin sped past him in the cruiser and blocked his path, Officer Newlen chased him on foot. Griffin said McDade was about to run past the police car but then turned and ran directly toward the cruiser, where Griffin was sitting. Griffin later said he was afraid that the teen was about to pull out a gun and shoot him. So Griffin opened fire. His partner Newlen heard the gunshots and thought McDade had opened fire on Griffin, so he also shot at McDade. The teen was hit seven times and killed. He wasn't armed.

The district attorney later ruled that the controversial shooting was justified because the officers had been led to believe McDade was armed. And Carrillo, the theft victim who called in the erroneous report, eventually pled guilty to filing a false report. He was sentenced to 90 days in jail.

Though McDade's case may seem extreme to some, it demonstrates the vulnerability of a potential suspect. Once the officers find a reason to put you in their car, your life could drastically, horribly transform in an instant, because you are now entering "the system." From this point on, anything might happen—a multitude of possible scenarios, each dependent on the actions and the decisions and, too often, the whims of others. Everything is now beyond your control. You have been thrown into America's prison-industrial complex: our version of human flypaper.

Once you are placed in that squad car, the likelihood is that you're going to jail. But most people, particularly those who don't have much interaction with the criminal justice system and law enforcement—though in many black communities a black male with no such interaction would be nearly impossible to find— don't see it yet. They think they just need to figure out the right thing to say to clear it all up. *I just need to show these cops that they've made a mistake. Then they'll let me go.*

So they open their mouths and launch into explanations: *I was just at the barbershop…I was on my way to get my daughter…I was just trying to catch the bus.*

But the officers aren't trying to hear any of that. You're going to the precinct.

"Tell it to your public defender," they might say. Or "Tell it to the judge."

I will go into more detail on this in the next chapter, but *the* most important thing any suspect must do in this situation can be summarized in four words: Shut the hell up!

If you are under some sort of delusion that the officer is your friend, or if they have taken a sweet tone with you to entice you to start talking, you must resist. Because the only things your words will do is get you into more trouble. The police will try to get some sort of statement from you, but if you're not even aware of the particulars of the crime they're investigating or they have accused you of committing, then you can't possibly determine whether your words will help you or hurt you.

I am aware of how unfair, how arbitrary, how painful this entire process can be. And how enraging. But at this point it becomes crucial for you to hold it together. You must exercise some discipline and self-control. Your most dominant impulse might be to strike out at the cops, to exhibit your anger and frustration, to show them how unfair it all is. But that would be exceedingly unwise. If they are loading you into the squad car because they think you've just committed a crime, then your anger and frustration, in their eyes, might be translated as guilt and desperation. In addition, you don't want to give them a reason to file any more charges against you—or worse, to hurt you. We have the voices of young men like Chavis Carter coming to us from the grave, telling us the extreme harm that can come in the back of that squad car.

Carter, 21, was killed by a gunshot wound to the head while handcuffed in the back of a police car in Arkansas. His case drew considerable outrage because the police claimed Carter shot himself in the head with a gun the police had apparently missed when they searched him. Carter's family is entirely unconvinced of the likelihood that the young man, with his hands cuffed behind his head, somehow managed to shoot himself in the right temple— particularly because he was left-handed. But that's what was determined by the Arkansas crime lab, which released an autopsy report stating that Carter committed suicide in that squad car. The report also added that Carter tested positive for methamphetamine, plus trace amounts of the anti-anxiety medication diazepam, the painkiller oxycodone, and marijuana.

In the United States, we have a very important document called the US Constitution. It includes a set of amendments, several of which are going to be of vital importance to you should you end up in police custody. The Fourth Amendment grants you the right to be free of unreasonable searches and seizures. It will be the job of your attorney to determine whether any of your rights have been violated. You also have the right to not lose your life, your liberty (your liberty being the ability to walk free in the streets), or your property without due process of law. That's the Fifth Amendment. And finally, the Fourteenth Amendment gives each citizen the right to equal protection under our laws.

Those are really important protections. But too often in my experience, I have found that individuals are much too quick to give those protections away by opening their mouths and letting the words flow without an attorney being present. The Constitution does you no good unless you use it.

It's understandable what might be going through your mind at this point. You're thinking, *If I tell the police that I don't want to talk unless my attorney is present, then they will think I'm guilty.* Or, *If I just tell them the truth they will let me go.*

What you must understand is that the whole process you're going through is designed to *not* let you go. Remember, economies depend on this. The prison-industrial complex across the nation is designed to pick you up off the street, book you into jail, hold you in a cell, take you to court, get you to plead guilty, and send you to prison. That's the system's intelligent design. That's what police officers are there for. Don't get it twisted by thinking the system is desperately going to want to correct the mistake it made in slapping the handcuffs on your wrist. The system has no interest in protecting your rights and ensuring you make it home to your family.

In many jurisdictions, police officers actually have ticket quotas they are trying to meet. Officers and former officers in municipalities ranging from New York City and Los Angeles to Atlanta and Auburn, Alabama, have come forward to accuse their departments of enforcing quotas that put extreme pressure on them to make stops and arrests. We should assume that the practice is widespread—making it even less likely that an officer is going to take off the cuffs and let you go just because you're telling him he's making a mistake.

I know African-American lawyers at some of the biggest law firms in the country whose kids have been racially profiled. They couldn't let their kids drive Dad's fancy car to their expensive private school in the suburbs for fear the kids would get stopped and harassed. US Attorney General Eric Holder, the top law enforcement officer in the land, has talked about the conversations he has to have with his son about what to do when a police officer stops you—how you're supposed to behave. Getting pulled into the system can happen to any of us. When your skin is brown, neither your education, your money, nor your prestige is going to shield you or your children.

There are numerous ways African Americans become targets simply because of race. Many African-American men and women have had the experience of what has come to be called "shopping while black": when retailers see an African American shopping in their store as a likely thief, rather than a paying customer.

Barneys of New York and Macy's have actually been sued by customers. After nineteen-year-old Trayon Christian bought a $350 Ferragamo belt in Barneys, he claimed in his lawsuit, he was accosted by undercover NYPD officers. The police actually said to Christian that he "could not afford to make such an expensive purchase," according to his suit. He was arrested and detained, even though he was able to show the police the receipt, the debit card he used, and his identification.

Actor Robert Brown said he was marched through Macy's in handcuffs and held for an hour after being falsely accused of credit card fraud.

And of course, when one of the richest women in the world, Oprah Winfrey, gets the shopping-while-black treatment, it makes big headlines. Oprah said a clerk at a ritzy store in Zurich, Switzerland—where Oprah was attending the wedding of Tina Turner—refused to show her a $38,000 handbag, thinking it was too expensive for her.

I had my own shopping-while-black encounter a few years back, when I ordered a new cell phone from my carrier and then went to the carrier's store in midtown Atlanta to switch my memory card to my new phone. The young white man waiting on me said, in an accusatory tone, "Where did you get this phone from?"

I was startled by the question. Here I was, this articulate, professional black woman, and he was essentially asking whether I had stolen the phone.

My response was something like, "Huh?"

I should have said, "Boy, I got three degrees! I don't need to steal a damn thing."

But instead of going off on him, I was so shocked that I said, "Uh, well, I ordered it."

That was several years ago, but every time I think about it a slow burn courses through me all over again.

Even President Obama has recounted his experience with racial profiling, saying in July 2013 after the George Zimmerman acquittal, "There are very few African-American men in this country who haven't had the experience of being followed when they were shopping in a department store. That includes me. There are very few African-American men who haven't had the experience of walking across the street and hearing the locks click on the doors of cars. That happened to me—at least before I was a senator."

Ironically, racial profiling might lead retailers to miss real culprits. Jerome Williams, a business professor at Rutgers University who has studied marketplace discrimination, told the Associated Press that one study has shown that white women in their 40s engage in more shoplifting than other demographic groups. Williams said they don't get caught because they aren't being watched.

Statistics showing that black customers steal more "are not really an indication of who's shoplifting," Williams said. "It's a reflection of who's getting caught. That's a reflection of who's getting watched. It becomes a self-fulfilling prophecy."

Racial profiling can even harm the youngest of African-American children. A 2005 study by the Yale Child Study Center found that African-American children were about twice as likely to be expelled from preschool as Latino and Caucasian children, and more than five times as likely to be expelled as Asian-American children. Even when controlling for socioeconomic status, African-American students in all grades are suspended and expelled at two to three times the rate of white students, according to researchers.

In 1997, a study by the US Department of Education revealed that nearly 25 percent of all African-American male students were suspended at least once over a four-year period—despite a lack of evidence that African-American students engage in higher levels of disruptive behavior than other students. In fact, a 2002 study published in *The Urban Review* by researchers from the University of Indiana and University of Nebraska found that African-American students are far more likely than their white classmates to be punished for reasons that require the subjective judgment of a teacher or administrator—things like disrespect, excessive noise, and loitering, as opposed to more concrete or objective infractions like smoking, leaving without permission, and vandalism, infractions for which the research reveals that white students are more likely than black students to be disciplined. If the punishment is triggered by a subjective judgment on the part of somebody in the school, the blackness of the students is a trigger that portends doom.

And the consequences of these suspensions are severe, because it becomes the first step into what has been called the school-to-prison pipeline: 49 percent of students who entered high school with three suspensions on their record eventually dropped out of school, according to a study by Johns Hopkins University.

This leads us to an astounding statistic: Black male high school dropouts are 38 times more likely to be incarcerated than black males with a four-year college degree. That first suspension on the record of a four-year-old child could be the scarlet letter that eventually propels him into a jail cell. What a dramatically outsized role teachers can have in the lives of young people—and what a large role they unwittingly play in the prison-industrial complex, a system that has created circumstances in this country that have led to the destruction of our young.

The deeper you dig into the system, from the arrest all the way through to the plea bargain and the rules of probation, the more you find these systemic booby traps and tricks that suck in our kids. From the perspective of a defense attorney, it starts to feel like these poor black boys in the 'hood have no chance once they're sucked in, because there are so many ways the system is set up against them.

From what I've seen, education is the only escape, the only way to wriggle free from the traps. That young boy has to make a conscious decision, early on in his life, that he will devote himself to academic performance and educational attainment. Otherwise he doesn't really have a shot in hell. Middle-class black folk looking at this from afar will say, "Why should I have sympathy for black boys in the system? They must have done something wrong. Just don't commit any crimes and you'll be okay." But what I've seen is that things are rarely that simple; there's a huge amount of gray area there. Getting caught up in some trouble can be so easy. It doesn't necessarily mean you're a bad person.

We criminalize so much youthful behavior now; so many of the things that my generation got into when we were younger, things that were seen as almost innocent rites of passage, will now get you locked up. When I was a kid, if you got into a fight at school, maybe your parents were called, maybe the school gave you some sort of in-school suspension or after-school detention, and then you went on with your life. Now that's called *affray*, and it's considered a crime. You could conceivably get a citation and have to appear in a juvenile court for that, particularly if there are police officers patrolling the halls, which is also something my generation didn't have to contend with when we were in school.

I can't help but think back on my own school years because I was in fights all the time growing up. I was the black girl who was never going to back down. So when I went to public school I was constantly fighting. I remember after one particular fight the assistant principal actually gave me a ride home because he knew my dad. On the ride home, he told me I needed to show more control. But if I had grown up 30 years later, I probably would have been put into the system at some point, labeled a trouble-maker, and slapped with some sort of probation that sat over my head like an anvil, just waiting for me to mess up again to come crashing down and trigger a whole lot of bad news for me.

In criminalizing youthful indiscretions, society has allowed stereotyping and irrational fears of black children to result in public school systems where black children are much more likely than everyone else to be harshly punished for many actions that in previous years might not have even drawn disciplinary action from school authorities.

Racial profiling is a corrosive force that black people have to deal with in many aspects of our lives, but what can we do about it? Despite the presence of the black man in the White House, I don't think any of us in our lifetimes will see a time when black men don't elicit irrational fears on the part of white people, or when black women aren't looked at sideways when trying to purchase some crazily overpriced Birkin handbag. So what can we do about it?

I don't want to discount the stress that comes from shopping while black and having retailers look at you as a potential criminal, but I think we can agree that the stakes are so much higher for black males and their encounters with the criminal justice system. So that's where I will focus my advice.

As I've said, education is always going to be key for any black male trying to avoid being ensnared in the system. But when I say education, I'm not just talking about academic performance.

It is crucial for young black males to educate themselves as much as possible about search and seizure laws, about probable cause, and about the rules and regulations that control the actions of law enforcement.

As a brilliant example, let's take the Nation of Islam and its adherents. I have always been impressed by how hard the Nation worked during the emergence of the Black Power movement of the 60s and 70s to ensure that most northern urban black Muslims were knowledgeable about the law. And the cops knew this. Of course this is a generalization, but many law enforcement officers were very clear that if they were dealing with guys in the suits and bow ties, they'd better speak respectfully and closely follow the letter of the law. If they were going to slap handcuffs on a member of the Nation, they'd better be explicitly clear about the reason. Because that brother was likely going to be armed with up-to-date knowledge of his rights. I've been working in the system for nearly two decades in and around Atlanta, with its extremely large black population, and still rarely have seen many black Muslim clients going in and out of jail. They did (and by appearance still do) a magnificent job preparing their young men to move about safely in the streets, free from the harassment that plagues their non-Muslim brethren. And they have done that with education: by making sure each of them are knowledgeable, their reputation subsequently seeped into the consciousness of every police officer.

That is the ideal state we would like to see for all of our young black males—to have enough knowledge of their rights that the cops wouldn't dare harass them. That is one of the purposes of this book.

Look at what happened when the police in Oklahoma tried to search the tour bus of the rapper 2 Chainz. An officer pulled the bus over because of the clichéd "broken tail light." When the bus driver exited the vehicle, the police claimed they saw "evidence of drug use." But while the driver stood outside with the police, 2 Chainz and the bus occupants locked the door and refused to let the officers board the bus and search for drugs unless they obtained a search warrant.

Their refusal led to a nine-hour standoff, which involved the police at some point actually towing the bus and its occupants to a police training facility as they tried to secure a search warrant. Though police sources claimed they did find drugs, 2 Chainz steadfastly denied that there were any drugs on the bus. And the actions of the police seemed to back him up, as he and his entourage were arrested "on complaints of interfering with official process." No drug charges ever came.

"This shit will make u go crazy," 2 Chainz tweeted after it happened. "Our bus gets pulled [over once] a week and they always say 'I smell weed I need to search ur bus.' Sht gets tiring."

Because 2 Chainz understood the system and his rights, his refusal to give permission meant they had to come up with something other than *we heard there may be drugs on this bus* to justify that stop. When a good attorney gets hold of a case like that, the dismissal will come with a quickness. Somebody did a magnificent job educating 2 Chainz (or 2 Chainz did a good job of educating himself). Since he previously had drug charges dismissed and since he was 35 when it happened, he clearly had picked up the knowledge he needed along the way. If you're going to be a rapper touring the country on a bus, you need to know the search and seizure laws. If more young black men were as prepared as 2 Chainz to deal with the system, it would be more difficult for them to be prosecuted in massive numbers.

A young black male recently met with me to discuss retaining my services. He had gotten stopped while driving on the highway; the police officer alleged that he had been driving erratically. The officer asked for permission to search his car; the young man gave him permission. Big mistake. The police went into his trunk and searched inside a suitcase, which exceeded what they should have been permitted to search. They found marijuana in excess of an ounce—felony level. This young man had just graduated from college with a B.S. degree.

All that education, but he wasn't knowledgeable about his rights, which could wind up rendering his degree unusable.

There are many variables to consider when the police pull you over, but there is a basic set of facts you must know if you're going to protect yourself.

Chapter 2: Silence Is Golden

How to Handle Stop-and-Frisk and Illegal Searches

FOR BLACK MALES, it is one of the most stressful, daunting situations they will ever encounter: getting pulled over by the police in their car or questioned by police while on foot. The trauma is extreme, even when they are innocent of any wrongdoing. They know that the wrong move, the wrong word, the wrong expression on their face can mean at least a night or two—and perhaps many more—stashed away in some horrible jail cell. In more than a few tragic cases, it has even meant death.

The stop is the logical consequence of racial profiling. As I've said before, the officer must have a reasonable and articulable suspicion that criminal activity is afoot. If he doesn't, then according to the law he shouldn't have made the stop. This is one of the most arguable points in the entire criminal justice system—the legality of the stop. Because of its importance, I'd like to bring you back to the beginning: the US Supreme Court decision covering this area of the law. To understand how we got to the place we are today, it's vital to comprehend how this all started.

The Supreme Court famously weighed in on the constitutionality of police stops in 1968 in its landmark *Terry v. Ohio* decision. The case involved a veteran Cleveland police detective, Martin McFadden, who saw three men acting in a manner he deemed "suspicious" while he was patrolling his beat in downtown Cleveland on October 31, 1963. When the officer approached the men, one of whom was John W. Terry, McFadden identified himself as a policeman and asked their names. After they "mumbled something," McFadden proceeded to pat Terry down and felt a pistol in his overcoat pocket. He ordered the men into a store, removed Terry's overcoat, and took out the revolver. He also seized a revolver from a second man, Richard Chilton. Terry and Chilton were subsequently charged with carrying concealed weapons.

The defense attorney representing Terry and Chilton tried to suppress the use of the seized weapons as evidence on grounds that the search and subsequent seizure were a violation of the Fourth Amendment. The court denied the motion and admitted the weapons into evidence, ruling that since the officer had cause to believe that Terry and Chilton were acting suspiciously, their interrogation was warranted, and that the officer, for his own protection, had the right to pat down their outer clothing, because he had reasonable cause to believe that they might be armed.

After Terry and Chilton were found guilty, their appeals eventually made their way to the US Supreme Court. In an 8–1 decision, written by Chief Justice Earl Warren—among the justices who joined his decision was Thurgood Marshall—the court ruled the Fourth Amendment prohibition against unreasonable searches and seizures is not violated when a police officer stops a suspect on the street and frisks him or her without probable cause, as long as the officer has a reasonable suspicion that the suspect has committed, is committing, or is about to commit a crime and has a reasonable belief that the person "may be armed and presently dangerous."

The court ruled that the police, for their own protection, may perform a quick surface search of the suspect's outer clothing for weapons if they have reasonable suspicion that the suspect is armed. According to the court, this reasonable suspicion must be based on "specific and articulable facts" and not merely upon an officer's hunch.

Importantly, in his concurring opinion, Justice Byron White pointed out that although the police may direct questions at a person they have stopped under the proper circumstances, "the person stopped is not obliged to answer, answers may not be compelled, and refusal to answer furnishes no basis for an arrest, although it may alert the officer to the need for continued observation."

After this decision, which set a precedent for a wide range of Fourth Amendment cases, the police search has come to be known in legal parlance as a *Terry* frisk, or a *Terry* stop when it applies to traffic stops.

As Justice White noted, a person is not obligated to answer the questions of the police when stopped. The importance of this point can't be overstressed. With this in mind, the worst thing that a black male can do when stopped is give the officer any verbal assistance whatsoever in demonstrating that he is a potential suspect. In other words, when stopped by police, the one thing that most people should do is be quiet. I understand that is the exact opposite of what human nature and our extreme desire to escape the situation compel us to do: talk.

In a remarkably high number of cases, potential suspects inadvertently give police tons of incriminating evidence that can be used against them simply because they try to talk themselves out of the situation, wrongly believing that if they just say the right thing, the police will let them go. But that is rarely the case. Many people talk themselves *into* criminal charges, rather than out of them. That is why we call this chapter "Silence Is Golden," because silence is the best response when stopped by the police— but it is the response least likely to be given.

While the Fourth Amendment protects US citizens against unreasonable searches and seizures, the Fifth Amendment guarantees the right to not lose our life or our liberty without due process of law. It is through the Fifth Amendment that the right to remain silent was born. This right has been the subject of some of the most hotly contested litigation in criminal cases, a right that was first articulated by the Supreme Court in the 1966 opinion on *Miranda v. Arizona*. (When Miranda confessed to the kidnapping and rape of a woman, the US Supreme Court threw out his conviction because his attorneys rightfully asserted that he should have been advised of his Fifth Amendment right to silence, among other rights. Thus was born the *Miranda* warnings.) Recently the US Supreme Court endangered that right in its troubling *Salinas v. Texas* decision, upholding a conviction where evidence was admitted of a defendant who appeared uncomfortable with police officers' questions, which the court ruled waived his right to remain silent.

This is one of the most crucial moments in the criminal-justice apparatus—what to do and say when stopped by the police. There are so many confusing rulings and bad advice floating around that it is hard to know the exact proper response in each situation.

To cut through the confusion, I have compiled this guide to help readers stay as safe as possible during the trauma of a police stop. Of course this is general advice and not intended to be construed as legal counsel, which should be obtained from your own attorney. Nor can I assure you that it will protect you in all circumstances, under all conditions. But it is information with which we all should be familiar.

What to Do If Stopped while Driving

- Pull over safely to the side of the road if you see a police car with flashing lights behind you
- If the officer asks where you're coming from, politely ask why you were stopped—the Supreme Court has ruled that the officer must have a reasonable suspicion based on "specific and articulable facts" that a person is armed or has committed, is committing, or is about to commit a crime
- Answer the officer's questions as succinctly as possible, without embellishment
- Always have your identification handy; if the officer asks for your license and registration, get his permission to reach for them— you don't want him thinking you may be reaching for a weapon
- If they ask for permission to search your car, politely refuse
- If the officer tells you to get out of the car, do as he says—and if he puts you up against the car, *stay there*
- If the police insist on searching the vehicle, remain silent while they are doing so
- Most importantly—though you will certainly be outraged— don't give the cop any attitude, or any reason to claim you were hostile or difficult, because that's the quickest way to escalate the encounter

What to Do If Stopped while Walking

- No matter what, never run from the police
- Police have the right to stop you and ask your name, so if this happens, politely tell them your name
- Beyond that initial question, remember the US Constitution guarantees each of us the right to remain silent, so don't volunteer any additional information
- Because the stop is usually a pretext for the officer to have close contact with you to see if you are under the influence of alcohol or illegal drugs, or in possession of contraband, be as polite and courteous as possible

- Don't curse or antagonize the officer
- There is a good chance the officer is stopping you because he believes you match the description for a suspect who did something nearby—such as a young black male with short hair. If that's the case, you won't be able to talk your way out of it—so don't say anything

What to Do If Arrested

- Be polite and don't contradict the officer's reason for arresting you
- Try to stay calm and resist the urge to become loud or aggressive
- Use every ounce of your willpower to resist the urge to say something to get them to release you—it's not going to happen, and will likely just make things worse
- As soon as you can, call someone who can hire you an attorney to come to the station as soon as possible
- If your parents or family members come to assist you, resist the urge to explain to them everything that happened—the police are likely recording every word you say to them

What to Do If You See Police Harassing a Friend

- Don't confront the police
- Your primary job is to get your friend to remain as calm and nonthreatening as possible. Keep telling him, "Calm down and be quiet"
- Create some distance between you and the police so they don't perceive you as dangerous
- As surreptitiously as possible, turn on the recording device on your cell phone. Having a video or audio recording of the encounter may become extremely important
- Do not intervene, because there's nothing you can do except escalate the encounter and make it worse
- Make sure you get the badge number of the officer involved

(A version of this list first appeared in the November 2013 issue of Ebony *magazine)*

The city of New York recently was the scene of a fascinating federal trial that probed the constitutionality of the controversial New York Police Department (NYPD) policy known as stop-and-frisk, which exploded during the administration of Mayor Michael Bloomberg. An outgrowth of the "broken windows" theory of policing that infiltrated the NYPD during the administration of Mayor Rudolph Giuliani, stop-and-frisk is based on the idea that if the NYPD stops individuals in high-crime areas to search for weapons and illicit items, thus taking guns off the streets, they can prevent them from being used in more serious crimes. In other words, stop-and-frisk should stop petty criminals from breaking windows before their behavior escalates into more serious crime.

Because racial profiling and stop-and-frisk tactics have become so commonplace in municipalities across the nation, it is vital to take a deep look at the proceedings in New York City since the legal dramas there will likely be used as precedent for the entire country. Though some of this may seem like too much "legalese" for some readers, I want you to be as well versed on the law as possible.

After Bloomberg took office in January 2002, the stop-and-frisk tactic took off. Between January 2004 and June 2012, the NYPD conducted 4.4 million stops, but just 6 percent resulted in arrests and 6 percent generated summonses, according to data compiled by the New York Civil Liberties Union. That means in 88 percent of the 4.4 million stops, the person stopped was doing nothing wrong. And while more than half of all people stopped were frisked, only 1.5 percent of the frisks uncovered weapons.

Blacks and Hispanics were stopped in 83 percent of the cases, although they make up just over half the New York City population.

It was this racial aspect of the stops that drew the most significant legal challenges. The Center for Constitutional Rights (CCR), a New York City-based nonprofit, started the ball rolling with a suit that resulted in a 2003 settlement that, among other things, required the NYPD to maintain a racial-profiling policy that complied with state and federal constitutions and to provide stop-and-frisk data to the CCR on a quarterly basis from 2003 to 2007. Based on the data yielded from that four-year period, another suit was filed against the NYPD, claiming its stop-and-frisk policies continued to violate the constitutional rights of black and Hispanic men.

In August 2013, US District Court Judge Shira Scheindlin delivered a scathing decision that lashed city officials who had "turned a blind eye" to evidence that officers carried out searches in a "racially discriminatory manner," thus violating individuals' right to privacy and equal treatment under the law.

"In their zeal to defend a policy that they believe to be effective, they have willfully ignored overwhelming proof that the policy of singling out 'the right people' is racially discriminatory and therefore violates the United States Constitution," the judge wrote.

Scheindlin said the unconstitutional stops have exacted a "human toll" in demeaning and humiliating law-abiding citizens.

In response, city officials continually argued that the racial disparity is justified because blacks and Hispanics commit more crimes, but Scheindlin summarily rejected that argument.

"This reasoning is flawed because the stopped population is overwhelmingly innocent—not criminal," she wrote. "There is no basis for assuming that an innocent population shares the same characteristics as the criminal suspect population in the same area."

Scheindlin's ruling essentially had two parts: (1) She said the city was not in compliance with what is required under the Constitution; and (2) She addressed the question of what to do about it by appointing a monitor to oversee the NYPD's compliance.

The ruling is extraordinary because while African Americans have endured racial profiling for centuries, feeling the nasty bite of the police officer's contempt, there is now legal precedent to support the contention that law enforcement singles out African Americans and Hispanics for special treatment. I would contend that wherever there are African Americans and police officers co-existing in the same place, there will be questions about the legality of many police stops. The police will strive to create a proxy to allow them to have contact with African-American males so that they can get to that place called reasonable and articulable suspicion.

Even before Scheindlin's ruling, the number of stops by the NYPD dropped by 57 percent in the first half of 2013, demonstrating that the legal challenge was already having an impact on the behavior of the police department. However, even though legal rulings in New York and California tend to be the most influential in the nation, I don't expect that Scheindlin's decision will cause police departments outside of New York City to substantially alter their policing tactics. Officers will continue to make questionable stops—that's the nature of the beast. They do it every day; they will continue to do it every day. But what Scheindlin's ruling says is that if a city has a policy, whether it is written or de facto (meaning it occurs in fact), that results in a disproportionate impact on a protected group like African Americans, it can be attacked in court and the jurisdiction might find itself subject to potential remedies such as those imposed in New York City. Even if you claim that it is unintentional, if you are in fact disproportionately stopping anyone of a protected class, the act could be seen as a violation of the Fourth and Fourteenth Amendments.

Essentially, the judge in New York has affirmed that the discrimination claimed by African Americans for many decades is not a figment of our imaginations. I expect that some savvy lawyers across the country will now start looking more closely at localities and start initiating lawsuits to challenge the constitutionality of their policing.

Of course, challenging stops on a racial basis really only works in the aggregate. Scheindlin's ruling is not going to be very helpful in challenging an individual stop as racially discriminatory. An attorney will have a very difficult time arguing that a particular officer was motivated by racism when stopping a particular African-American male. If the officer claims that the male was driving in an erratic way or was driving with a broken tail light, or if the officer claims he smelled the odor of marijuana as he walked up to the car, it will always be challenging to use race in the defense.

Officers are trained to follow a cookie-cutter script that largely insulates them from attack. It is very difficult for an attorney to get a court to agree that a stop is illegal and should be thrown out. That rarely happens. With stops, much of what we are discussing sits comfortably under the banner of subjectivity. So what needs to change, what a ruling like Scheindlin's needs to impact, is what occurs in the mind of a police officer before a stop is made. When that officer spots a black or Hispanic male, what are the thoughts that will race through his mind? Scheindlin reasoned that because the overwhelming majority of African Americans or Hispanics are innocent of any crimes, an officer has no basis for assuming any African American or Hispanic that he sees is a potential criminal—even if the majority of the criminals in the area are African American or Hispanic.

I will repeat Scheindlin's words because they essentially serve as the antithesis to every act of racial profiling that has ever been committed: "There is no basis for assuming that an innocent population shares the same characteristics as the criminal suspect population in the same area."

In other words, **if you are a police officer who stops someone simply because he is the same color and gender as the majority of the criminals you have arrested, you have just violated the US Constitution.** I put that in bold because it is a thought I believe each of us needs to carry around in our heads, regardless of our skin color. In fact, I laid out the details of the New York City case primarily so that you would truly understand and remember the context of the above sentence.

At times, the overzealousness of police officers can appear almost silly to observers. Take, for instance, the case of Jasper Boyd, a 52-year-old Brooklyn father who in November 2011 left his apartment in a hurry to pick up his 7-year-old son from school. When Boyd realized it was raining outside, he quickly ducked back inside the building to get an umbrella; then he continued on his way.

Going back to get an umbrella certainly is a reasonable activity with which we can all identify—"reasonable" unless you happen to be a black male in certain neighborhoods in the US. Boyd was moving a little too quickly for Officer Wilson Gonzalez of the NYPD. The officer stepped to Boyd and stopped him. Boyd produced his ID and told Gonzalez he had gone inside to get an umbrella. When the officer told Boyd he wanted to run his identification to see if he had any outstanding warrants for his arrest, Boyd—a former corrections officer—protested. Gonzalez began to frisk him and eventually charged him with disorderly conduct.

But Boyd wouldn't let the matter sit. After he picked up his son, he went down to the local precinct to file a complaint against Gonzalez. When the case finally made it to the independent Civilian Complaint Review Board two years later, Officer Gonzalez pleaded guilty to a wrongful stop-and-frisk and also to writing the summons "without sufficient legal authority."

If approved by the police commissioner, the officer could lose 15 days' pay as punishment.

Boyd's response to the wrongful stop was precisely what should be done in the situation—obey the officer's request to see your ID, but put pressure on the system by filing a formal complaint, even if the system tries to make it difficult for you. When Boyd went to the Brooklyn precinct, he was told that they didn't have any more complaint forms, according to media reports. But Boyd would not be deterred.

A more troubling response to a police stop was exhibited by 39-year-old Oriana Ferrell, when she was pulled over for speeding in a van filled with her five children near Taos, New Mexico. Ferrell was on her way from their home in Tennessee to the Rio Grande on an educational trip with her children. Rather than obeying the officer who told her to wait until he checked her license, Ferrell, apparently frightened for the safety of her children, stepped on the gas and sped away. A video of the incident, recorded from the dashboard camera of the police car, went viral and was even shown on the *Today* show and other national news programs.

After she inexplicably drove away, the officer gave chase and pulled her over a second time. Visibly angry, the officer ran to the car, yelling, "Get out of the vehicle! Get out of the vehicle right now!"

When the officer actually tried to pull Ferrell out of the vehicle, her fourteen-year-old son got out of the van and valiantly ran over to defend his mom—until the officer aimed his Taser at the boy, sending him back inside the van.

"Sir, I pulled back over, I didn't run away," Ferrell pleaded. "You see my children. I'm not doing anything wrong. I'm just trying to take them to the Rio Grande."

The mother and the son struggled with the officer before getting back in the minivan. The officer then used his baton to violently smash the passenger side window where the fourteen-year-old boy was sitting. When Ferrell again took off in her van, a second officer fired at least three shots at the vehicle filled with children. Even if Ferrell's actions were bizarre, many observers were stunned that an officer who clearly was not in any danger himself would fire on a van filled with children.

Ferrell was arrested and charged with child abuse, fleeing an officer, and possession of drug paraphernalia—the police found what they claimed were two marijuana pipes in the car. The fourteen-year-old was charged with battery. But the officer who shot at the van, Elias Montoya, was fired by the New Mexico State Police.

While Ferrell's actions were wrong, they clearly didn't warrant Officer Montoya's response. Not everyone who encounters the police or strangers in public is going to be mentally stable or completely rational—but that shouldn't result in a death sentence. That's what happened to nineteen-year-old Renisha McBride when she stumbled onto the porch of Theodore Wafer in Dearborn Heights, Michigan, in the wee hours of the morning after she crashed her car: Wafer opened fire with his shotgun through his closed front and screen doors and blasted her in the face, killing her.

That's also what happened to former Florida A&M football player Jonathan Ferrell, 24, who was gunned down by Charlotte, NC, police when he approached officers for help after his car hit a tree.

And of course seventeen-year-old Trayvon Martin was killed while walking down the street with a pack of Skittles and a can of iced tea—those are the basic facts, despite the jury verdict of not guilty for shooter George Zimmerman.

It devastates me that here in the second decade of the twenty-first century, we are still seeing young people killed under these ridiculous circumstances. Young people gunned down without dignity, without regard to the lack of malice in their hearts. Lives stolen away in 2013—as if we were still in 1930 or even 1830. Needless. Senseless. Outrageous.

Chapter 3: The History between Police and Black Males

From Slave Patrols to the KKK–to Today

AS AN ATTORNEY, I spend my days in the past. An attorney's world is preoccupied with precedent—how matters in the present were previously adjudicated. History is our guide, the controlling force dominating our actions. So when I consider the often-volatile relationship between African Americans and the police, it's only natural for me to look back, to ask myself how and when the relationship got so bad.

But that question isn't exactly the right one. A close reading of US history yields a stark fact: Law enforcement in the US has always been an enemy of black people.

To a large extent, law enforcement in the US, particularly in the American South, was *created* as a means to monitor, control, and punish black people. As a helpful guide on this shocking history, I turned to the work of Sally E. Hadden, one of the few scholars to explore this issue in depth. Her 2001 book, *Slave Patrols: Law and*

Violence in Virginia and the Carolinas, is a must-read for anyone who might be curious about the link between the enslavement of African Americans and origins of American law enforcement.

"The new American innovation in law enforcement during the eighteenth and early nineteenth centuries was the creation of racially focused law enforcement groups in the American South," Hadden writes in *Slave Patrols.* "The history of police work in the South grows out of this early fascination, by white patrollers, with what African American slaves were doing. Most law enforcement was, by definition, white patrolmen watching, catching, or beating black slaves."

Ever since Africans were dragged to these shores, black bodies have been treated by white society as a demonstrable threat, a simmering mass of anger and affront—close by and yearning for retribution.

With this history, should it be a surprise that the relationship between the police and African Americans, even 150 years after Emancipation, is characterized by fear and loathing, abuse and death?

Maya Angelou once said, "The more you know of your history, the more liberated you are." By tracing the straight line from slave patrols to post-Emancipation policing to the KKK to modern police forces, African Americans can better understand the nature of the relationship we currently suffer through with regard to law enforcement in the US. This understanding allows us to properly prepare our children, our black boys and girls, for the animosity they are likely to face from police when they step out from under their parents' watchful eye.

History can help save our lives.

Throughout the literature on slavery, one constant remains: the white community's ever-present fear.

In a published piece on Southern slave patrols, writer Philip L. Reichel describes legislation passed in Georgia as early as 1770 instituting the death penalty for slaves found guilty of even attempting to poison whites, which was necessary because "the detestable crime of poisoning hath frequently been committed by slaves," according to the legislature. Reichel also quotes a 1761 issue of the *Charleston Gazette*, which complained, "the Negroes have again begun the hellish practice of poisoning."

While poisonings were a more personalized form of retribution—capable of striking terror in the hearts of slave owners as they watched their bondsmen and bondswomen prepare their meals, fetch their water, and raise their children—it was the slave insurrections that truly evoked fears throughout the white community. After the Stono slave uprising in 1730 near Charleston resulted in the death of 40 blacks and 20 whites, the South Carolina legislature in 1740 established slave patrols. It said the patrols were necessary because of the "many late horrible and barbarous massacres" that have been committed against whites by blacks "who are generally prone to such cruel practices."

In *Slave Patrols*, Hadden writes that towns like Wilmington in North Carolina and Charleston in South Carolina created their own night-watch groups to control slave behavior.

"These night-watch groups constitute the forerunners of urban slave patrols and later the police," she writes. "Urban growth gave rise to new fears for Southern whites. Clustered together in houses and stores, people and goods concentrated in a town presented a tempting target for slaves bent on arson, vandalism, or theft... The date of a town settlement, its rate of population growth, and the number of slaves resident, all these factors will influence how soon town officials wanted a well regulated, paid city patrol."

The fears of Southern whites heightened considerably after the start of the Civil War, which conscripted able-bodied white men to fight for the Confederacy—and leave behind their plantations, where whites were dramatically outnumbered. It was a major preoccupation of Southern white men during the war years what might happen to their women, children, and plantations if they left the slaves untended. This fear led them to exempt from war duty any man who owned or supervised 20 slaves or more— an exemption that came to be known as the "20-nigger law." The law was tinkered with several times during the war to reduce the number of exemptions, but scholars still estimate that as much as 40 percent of the eligible adult male population was exempted from serving in the Confederate military.

After the war's end, newly freed slaves flocked into the cities of the South, where, as scholar Eric Foner put it, "many blacks believed 'freedom was freer.' Here were black social institutions— schools, churches, and fraternal societies—and here, too, in spite of inequities in law enforcement, were the army…and Freedmen's Bureau, offering protection from the violence so pervasive in much of the rural South."

Richmond's slave population exploded from an estimated 12,000 slaves in 1860 to 30,000 freedmen by 1865. Of course with this explosion in brown bodies came a dramatic increase in the fears of whites.

In Charlottesville, Virginia, Hadden writes, "city dwellers surrounded by multitudes of strange, unfamiliar freedmen stood in terror, waiting for the insurrection that never came."

The newly created Freedmen's Bureau, in addition to the Union army, had its hands full stepping into conflicts between the freedmen and the Southern police forces intent on using violence to control them. Union commanders even took the step of removing some police officers from duty in places like Wilmington, North Carolina, and Sumter, South Carolina, for using excessive force against blacks. In many places, police officers ravaged the homes of freedmen, taking for themselves whatever goods they wanted.

Hadden reports in *Slave Patrols* that in 1865, the head of a county police force in the Cape Fear region of North Carolina violently murdered four freedmen because they refused to turn over the crops they had planted and harvested on their former master's lands.

The fears of Southern whites were exacerbated by the news in November 1865 that blacks in the British West Indies had revolted. Many whites thought their days surely were numbered, particularly in states like South Carolina, where blacks outnumbered whites. Some scholars have even suggested that the reports of planned insurrections among blacks that were sweeping through white communities were merely calculated rumors started by whites intent on using them as an excuse to terrorize freedmen with their extralegal patrol groups.

After the Civil War, the violent methods of patrols would also be adopted and renewed by groups "dedicated to white supremacy at all costs, even by illegal means," Hadden writes. "The seemingly unrestricted brutality of patrols would find its mirror image during Reconstruction in the extralegal activities of vigilante groups that operated outside virtually all social restrictions. As slaves, bondsmen had often been protected from patrollers by their masters, who (for paternalistic or materialistic reasons) did not wish to have their 'property' damaged by roving slave patrols. With slavery's abolition and the end of property rights in slaves, freedmen found they had no guardians to protect them from the rebirth of patrol-like violence in the postwar period. White Southerners visited retribution upon freedmen who had little means of protecting themselves from the next incarnation of slave patrols: the Ku Klux Klan."

Southern whites, feeling frustrated by their powerlessness and emboldened by their vague fears of threat from newly freed blacks, flocked to join the KKK, which was started in 1865 in Tennessee. Whites quickly saw the vigilante group as a way to scare the freedmen into political and social submission. While slaves were protected from extreme violence by their status as the property of their white masters, that relationship was gone after Emancipation, as was their "protection."

In North Carolina counties like Caswell, Orange, and Alamance, the sheriff, deputies, and all important local officials were members of the Klan.

"Restraints upon mobility, socialization, and property ownership that slave patrols had legally imposed continued almost without interruption under the extralegal enforcement of the Klan," Hadden writes. "While patrollers inflicted 40 lashes, at most, to prevent slaves from moving around, the Klan readily shot or killed hundreds. Moreover, the KKK destroyed property and drove off workers who would have made their communities economically stronger. Former slaves and white Republicans found KKK coffins on their doorsteps, warning them to leave the South."

Hadden points out this curiosity: Even some of the language and methods of modern policing originated in the slave patrols. The word "beat" started as a means of describing the areas groups would patrol in South Carolina and other states, eventually becoming the police term for an officer's area of responsibility. The term "patrol" also came from the slave patrols. While Hadden concedes that these words were around before the creation of slave patrols, "their use in the context of law enforcement today owes much to their application in the slaveholding South."

In addition to language, practices such as "stakeouts" were adopted from the methods of slave patrollers.

When Reconstruction forced the slave patrols to adopt methods that appeared on the surface to be racially unbiased, law enforcement simply passed on the ruthless violence to the purview of the KKK, which Hadden notes "provided an outlet for the racial aggression that white Southerners could no longer legally inflict through patrolling or slave ownership."

In a February 2014 speech, US Attorney General Eric Holder, in making an appeal for states to allow ex-convicts to vote, pointed out how "many Southern states enacted disenfranchisement schemes to specifically target African Americans and diminish the electoral strength of newly freed populations."

"The resulting system of unequal enforcement—and discriminatory application of the law—led to a situation, in 1890, where ninety percent of the Southern prison population was black," Holder said. "And those swept up in this system too often had their rights rescinded, their dignity diminished, and the full measure of their citizenship revoked for the rest of their lives. They could not vote."

Into the 1900s, the targeting of African Americans by the police continued unabated. In a 1973 issue of the *Journal of Southern History*, Ohio State University professor Eugene J. Watts published an article called "The Police in Atlanta, 1890–1905" that recounted many examples of the police abusing and demeaning blacks. The article quotes former Atlanta Chief of Police John Ball stating that Atlanta was a law-abiding city except for "many petty offenses resultant from a large negro population." Chief Ball even asked that city authorities keep open "negro dives" and other places of poor reputation to make it more convenient for the police to use them as a means to "corral criminals."

In 1903, an editorial in the *Atlanta Constitution*, the local white newspaper, called for stiffer enforcement of the vagrancy law, aimed at "idle shiftless negroes—for the majority of the crimes punished in city court are committed by this class."

The point of view was decidedly different in Atlanta's black newspaper, the *Weekly Defiance*, which in 1881 published this statement: "We have lived in Atlanta twenty-seven years, and we have heard the lash sounding from the cabins of the slaves, poured on by their masters; but we have never seen a meaner set of low down cut throats, scrapes and murderers than the city of Atlanta has to protect the peace."

Another editorial in the *Weekly Defiance* in 1881 described policemen who enjoyed standing in the middle of the sidewalk and forcing black women to walk around them, thus deepening the hatred and hostility.

Institutional habits and practices get passed on from generation to generation. By deed and description, police veterans train the newbies, telling them and showing them what the bad guys look like, what they sound like, what they smell like. As decades pass and those rookies become wizened veterans, they repeat the same lessons to another generation. It doesn't take long to get us from the early 1900s to the Civil Rights Movement to today—just a few generations of policing.

If you're still skeptical, consider the math: The grandson of a police officer who joined the force at age 20 in Charleston or Atlanta or Boston in 1905 could wind up training officers in 1995 (with the assumption that the grandfather, his son, and his grandson each spent 30 years on the force)—passing along lessons his grandpa might have passed on to him from his days patrolling black neighborhoods at the turn of the century when the Klan was still growing in influence.

The twentieth century is so replete with instances of police abusing, targeting, and murdering African Americans that I could cover the rest of these pages trying to list all of them. In the early decades of the century, dozens of African Americans were lynched every year —an estimated 89 lynchings in 1908, 76 in 1919, 51 in 1922—often with the involvement of law enforcement. Cities like Atlanta, Philadelphia, East St. Louis, and Springfield, Illinois, exploded in deadly race riots—often triggered by some horrific act committed by a white police officer.

Music legend Quincy Jones, in his 2001 memoir *Q: The Auto-biography of Quincy Jones*, describes how the black community in Chicago in the 1940s had just as much to fear from black police officers as they did from white ones.

"Every weekend we watched a legendary black cop named Two-Gun Pete who carried two pearl-handled revolvers shoot black kids in the back in broad daylight, right in front of a Walgreens drugstore—the kids dropped like potato sacks," Jones writes. "We fantasized about making Two-Gun Pete pay."

Police played a role in some of the most well publicized instances of racist violence in our history—if not directly then indirectly. When fourteen-year-old Emmett Till was murdered by Mississippi racists in 1955, Tallahatchie County Sheriff Clarence Strider claimed Till's bloated and disfigured body, fished out of the Tallahatchie River, was a cadaver planted by the NAACP. Then Strider kept two black witnesses to the crime locked away in jail so they couldn't testify during the trial—a trial during which Strider would welcome black spectators with the greeting, "Hello, niggers!"

When civil rights workers James Earl Chaney, Andrew Goodman, and Michael Schwerner were killed in Mississippi in June 1964, among the perpetrators were members of the Neshoba County Sheriff's Office and the Philadelphia (Mississippi) Police Department, in addition to the Ku Klux Klan.

As we well know, controversial killings at the hands of police continued through the end of the twentieth century and into the new millennium. In fact, a 2013 report by a group called the Malcolm X Grassroots Movement concluded that police officers, security guards, or self-appointed vigilantes killed at least 313 African Americans in 2012, a rate of one every 28 hours.

In my legal practice, I see examples of police abuse so frequently that it could still be considered commonplace. So the proper question has never been, *When did the relationship between blacks and the police get so bad?* The more relevant question is, *Why hasn't the relationship ever gotten better?*

Some may ask whether it's fair to connect the current strained relations between African Americans and the police with the hostilities that existed 150 years ago, when African Americans were just limping out of slavery. I would propose that while the two sides definitely have the power to change the nature of the relationship in 2014, it's foolhardy to presume there is no link between the relationship now and the relationship then, particularly since interactions between the two sides have remained hostile through the years. It's like asking whether the current economic and social challenges of the African-American community have any connection to our previous condition of servitude. While we do have the power to change our conditions and break away from any shackles that still hold us down, there's no denying that American institutions remain aligned to promulgate the discrimination and oppression that have subjugated African Americans for centuries. African Americans' opportunities are vastly improved, but there are still systems in place to hold our community down. The criminal justice system is one of these systems.

One final note: This chapter is not meant to imply that *all* members of law enforcement are still actively conspiring to abuse and oppress African Americans, any more than a study of slavery's brutality is meant as an indictment of all white people in 2014. But this history is surely something all Americans need to be aware of when assessing the still-tense relationship between African Americans and the police.

Chapter 4: The Plea Bargain Trap

How to Fight It

IF THE PRISON-INDUSTRIAL COMPLEX were a living, breathing animal, and the police arrest was the oxygen that breathed life into the organism, then the plea bargain would be the blood rushing through its veins, allowing it to thrive. The plea bargain process sends a steady stream of bodies into the system, keeping the jobs secure and the money flowing.

In the US, 97 percent of federal cases and 94 percent of state cases never make it to trial. Instead, prosecutors and defense attorneys negotiate the resolutions to criminal charges against defendants in what is called a plea deal. This means a defendant admits guilt in exchange for some type of leniency in sentencing. He goes to jail without ever facing his accuser, and without ever having the charges against him thoroughly probed in a court of law.

Prison Profiteering is a 2013 investigative video series created by *The Nation* magazine, the ACLU, and Beyond Bars, an award-winning media campaign started by Brave New Films. It unveils the vast network of private corporations, states, and localities that benefit from America's massive prison system. *Prison Profiteering* details the myriad ways that the multibillion-dollar system profits from the incarceration of 2.3 million people—the greatest imprisonment system on Earth. The series includes a quote from Alex Friedmann, an editor at *Prison Legal News*, who likened the nation's prison-industrial complex to the hotel industry.

"The hotel industry wants to keep their beds full as much as possible, because it means more revenue," he said. "Same thing for the private prison companies."

When seen from this perspective, it's easy to view the US prison system as modern-day slavery: nameless, faceless black bodies employed on a massive scale to generate revenue for unseen oligarchs.

As part of this profit-making industry, the plea bargain has been honed into an essential tool to save the system time. It also happens to guarantee a steady supply of prisoners. Numerous studies have shown that black defendants fare much worse than white defendants in the plea bargain process, routinely receiving lengthier sentences than whites who are accused of the same crimes. In combination with the imposition of mandatory minimum sentences, the plea deal is one of the primary reasons why the black prison population has exploded while actual crime in the US has plummeted.

As Michelle Alexander reveals in her book, *The New Jim Crow*, prosecutors admit that they routinely "load up" charges against defendants, throwing at them a stack of crimes with harsh sentences—charges that the prosecutors know they wouldn't be able to prove in court—in order to force the defendants to plead guilty to lesser offenses. The nation's so-called War on Drugs gave prosecutors the tools to put extreme pressure on defendants, with the long mandatory minimum sentences for dealing and even possession of crack cocaine that Congress imposed in 1986.

This is all part of the grand design, as the US Sentencing Commission conceded in its 1991 report to Congress, in which it concluded that "the value of a mandatory minimum sentence lies not in its imposition, but in its value as a bargaining chip to be given away in return for the resource-saving plea from the defendant to a more leniently sanctioned charge."

But even the Sentencing Commission noted the racial disparities in the plea bargain process in the same report to Congress:

"The disparate application of mandatory minimum sentences in cases in which available data strongly suggest that a mandatory minimum is applicable appears to be related to the race of the defendant, where whites are more likely than non-whites to be sentenced below the applicable mandatory minimum; and to the circuit in which the defendant happens to be sentenced, where defendants sentenced in some circuits are more likely to be sentenced below the applicable mandatory minimums than defendants sentenced in other circuits."

Plea bargains are the expected result for the drug cases that flood most of the nation's courts. Marijuana possession arrests clog the system's arteries like a fast-food snack—easy and cheap and almost impossible to avoid. I see an unending stream of these possession cases, where the accused are caught with quantities great enough to be considered felonies but less than trafficking. For a first offense, the prosecutors will offer something in the neighborhood of 3–5 years of probation. Such an offer looks extremely enticing to defendants, even those who are loudly proclaiming their innocence, because it means they avoid prison time.

But it also means that if they get arrested and caught up in the system again, or if they commit one of the acts that is considered a probation violation—which, tragically, is extremely likely in many of our communities—they will find themselves behind bars. In some cases, they might get hit for something as simple as failing to pay the fine in a timely fashion.

In my experience, with drug cases it's important to know the facts before you start mulling over plea bargains. Drug cases are very fact-sensitive, meaning the details are crucial. For instance, when a car full of black males gets pulled over and the police get permission to search the vehicle, or claim they have a "reasonable, articulable suspicion" that criminal activity is afoot, everybody in the car usually gets charged if any drugs are found hidden anywhere in the vehicle, such as under a seat. In these circumstances, it's typical that nobody in the car is willing to take responsibility for the drugs. The cop will hold up the bag of weed and everybody will start looking crazy and saying, "It's not mine!" In response, the police just slap the cuffs on every passenger in the car.

(On rare occasions, the driver might say, "Yeah, those were my drugs"—usually if one of the passengers is a young family member or friend he badly wants to protect from a criminal record.)

When all the passengers get charged with possession, depending on their criminal record everybody's likely to get the same offer—5 years on probation. Younger defendants might get even more stringent, intensive probation requirements to "keep them in line." The system thinks this more stringent probation is necessary to discourage younger defendants—but this also makes it easier for them to violate the terms of their probation.

But that probated sentence might have been absolutely the wrong decision for the passengers in the above scenario. If you're a passenger in that car, in the front seat or even in the back seat, you have a good argument that you were not in control of the drugs, that they don't belong to you, and that you didn't even know they were there. But if you take that plea deal, then you're admitting guilt without the state having to prove it. That could come back to haunt you in a hurry.

Experts estimate that 2 to 5 percent, and probably more, of the people currently in prison are innocent, largely because of the plea-bargain system. This means tens of thousands of innocent people, a huge majority of them black and brown men, are languishing in prison cells where, as Michelle Alexander notes, "some will die."

The role of the defense attorney is vital during this plea negotiation process. I try hard not to influence a client's decision about whether to take a plea. I think pushing a client in a particular direction is a dangerous place for an attorney to find herself. Invariably a client will, at some point, become dissatisfied that he took a plea, particularly if he later violates the probation and winds up behind bars. When that happens, the first place his finger will point is directly at his attorney.

I try to get my clients to take ownership of their actions, whichever way they choose to go with the plea offer. If they choose to go to trial, they do so taking ownership of their assertion of innocence. If they take the plea, they do so with full knowledge of the ramifications of that action. Yes, often they are just begging me to provide guidance, to tell them what to do. What they want is some idea of certainty of the outcome. They want me to assure them what the result will be if we go to trial. But that's the last thing a knowledgeable and responsible attorney should be doing. I always preface any discussion of a possible trial by telling the client I have no control over what a jury will do. But I feel comfortable telling the client whether the facts of the case strongly indicate his innocence. Whether the jury will properly see and consider those facts is something I can't predict.

The facts are the facts; you can't change them. Sometimes the facts force you to have a very grown-up conversation with your client, to tell him: "These are the facts in your case that hurt you, and these are the facts that help you." This allows him to make an informed decision about a plea bargain. There are attorneys out there who will tell a client, "I can absolutely get you off on this charge." But I believe that's dangerous. It unnecessarily raises the level of expectation in a client or a client's family. If things don't work out the way everyone expects, these people will be soured on the legal profession forever. There will be no redeeming it.

My motivation here is not to protect the legal profession. I'm trying to get my clients to be able to make their own decisions. As humans, we are quick to turn around and blame somebody else for our troubles or problems, rather than owning our own stuff. As part of my practice, I try to get my clients to own their own stuff by being fully informed.

I recently had a young client who asserted his innocence after being charged with armed robbery. The prosecutor offered him a sentence of 15 years, with 10 served in prison. Fortunately the facts of the case were in his favor. The victim ID'd my client through a friend's Facebook page—with the friend stating "that's the guy," though this "friend" was not present during the robbery. Every attorney is obligated to tell the client what the prosecutor assigned to the case has offered in terms of a plea deal. I always further state: "If you decide you want to go to trial and the jury does not agree with the facts as we see them, then ultimately you are the one who has to do the time in prison. I am going to walk away and go home. So you have to be the one to make the decision."

My client decided to go to trial, knowing that if we lost, he'd be looking at a likely sentence in excess of 40 years in prison. In this case, we were fortunate that the prosecutor dismissed the charges. Some observers might say that my approach is a very cold and clinical way to deal with clients. But I prefer to think of it as honest. It is addressing clients as the adults they are, and making sure they understand that the plea decision belongs to them and no one else.

There are times when a client may assert his innocence, but the facts are so overwhelmingly against him that I have to try to shake him out of his delusion. I had one client who insisted on going to trial to fight armed robbery and other charges, but numerous people identified him as the person who broke into a restaurant after hours and locked the employees in a cooler while he robbed the place. He was looking at 3 counts of armed robbery, 6 counts of aggravated assault, and a count of kidnapping (a potential sentence in excess of 100 years), and he was being offered a deal of 15 years in prison.

"You need to man up," I told him. "You know there are all these facts against you."

"I want to talk to my mother," he said.

He was in custody, so there was no way I could connect him to his mother.

"What would your mother say to you?" I asked him. "Would she say something to the effect of, 'You need to man up?'"

Part of the deal was that they were letting his younger brother go free. His brother had been charged solely because my client used his brother's cell phone during the crime. The younger brother had no prior record, so they were kicking him free.

After much anguish and denial, my client finally said, "You're right, I *do* need to man up."

I'm not in a position to say my client was lying when he asserted his innocence, but I will say the facts were overwhelmingly against him, pointing to an almost certain guilty verdict at trial.

One of the things I find most frustrating about the plea-bargain system—in addition to the racial disparity in the sentencing and plea offers—is that the generosity of the plea offer greatly depends on where the alleged crime was committed, just as the US Sentencing Commission conceded in its 1991 report to Congress. I see it all the time in Georgia, where an armed robbery is an automatic 20-year sentence—partly in prison and partly on probation—outside the Atlanta metro area, but in urban courts, the same charge will likely bring a sentence of just 10 years. So as I sit there talking to a client in one of the rural counties, it's frustrating to know that his sentence could be cut in half if we were inside the Atlanta perimeter.

That's terribly unfair, but it's the system we have, and I don't see it changing any time soon.

Another concern when contemplating a plea offer is whether you are represented by a public defender. Due primarily to the sheer number of cases they must handle, public defenders are not able to spend as much time on each case as private attorneys do. So there may be a greater tendency on their part to grab a plea offer than if a private retained attorney were handling the same case. Listen very closely to the words the public defender uses when describing the plea offer to you. If your attorney (either a public defender or private attorney) is telling you that you will lose at trial and do 40 years in prison so you better take the plea, but you think they know less about the facts of your case than you do, then you should be asking a lot of questions about why your counsel is so sure you will be convicted. Make sure his recommendation is not just a matter of convenience, a way to quickly get your case off his to-do list.

In an armed robbery case where I was a private attorney and the co-defendant was represented by a public defender, my client was adamant about his innocence and wanted to go to trial. But the public defender was pushing the co-defendant to take a plea. After having the talk, I followed my client's wishes and prepared the case for trial. On the day we began the trial, the other attorney told me that her client was going to testify against my client. When she walked away from her client for a few minutes, I leaned over and asked him whether it was true that he was testifying against my client.

He looked at me like I was crazy.

"No, there's nothing to testify about," he said. "We didn't do anything."

I had come up with a very strong presentation for the trial. The public defender had not. Ultimately the jury acquitted both of them. But that case still haunts me because it makes me wonder how often something like that happens, where the public defender (or a bad private attorney) will actually lie to encourage someone to take a plea if there's no one around who will look closely at the facts, do the research, and present a case.

In my experience, there aren't a lot of attorneys who will go the extra mile to do all of that. The tragedy of the system is that when diligent research and investigation doesn't happen, many young men will languish in prison who didn't have to be there, who could be home living their lives if the attorney had just pushed to present a real case rather than taking the first offer that came his or her way.

This is where the economic investment comes in for defendants, as I will talk about in more detail in the next chapter on hiring an attorney. Do you stay with a public defender (or private attorney) who is encouraging you to take a plea, even though you believe yourself to be innocent? If you're not delusional or under the supervision of a psychiatrist, you need to do everything in your power to make sure you have someone representing you who is going to pursue your innocence as if her own freedom depended on it.

Over the years, I have found that I've become less interested in whether I believe a client is guilty or innocent. Attorneys go through an evolutionary process when they join the bar. Being a trial attorney is a journey, not a destination. You are constantly learning new things and growing as a litigator. Eventually you get to this place where the client's actual guilt or innocence is a small part of the whole equation. The key question becomes: Can the state sustain their burden and prove guilt beyond a reasonable doubt?

Ultimately I don't care whether my client did it or not. That's not what I'm there for. I leave that judgment to God. My job is to hold the state to its burden. I do realize that this kind of thinking may turn some people's stomachs and contribute to the negative perception many people have of defense attorneys. Everybody wants to judge; everybody wants others to be judged. But when you're an advocate for a client, it's not your job to judge.

Chapter 5: Get Me Johnnie Cochran

When You Don't Have Cash to Hire a High-Profile Lawyer

FOR MOST PEOPLE, the first time they get arrested is a terrifying experience, filled with uncertainty, confusion, and fear of what's to come. The portrayals in the media of prison life, both fictional and real, paint a picture of humiliation, violence, and rape.

It's no wonder then that people in these circumstances see their attorney as a sort of life raft—the only person who can save them, maybe even return their life to normalcy. Families are often compelled to unload all their fears and insecurities onto the attorney, expecting in return that the attorney will instantly transform into a therapist and social worker.

I am aware of these expectations when I take on a new criminal client. So even though I know the client and likely his family too are in a very fragile and emotionally explosive state, in order for me to do my job effectively, I have to make it clear up front that I am not the family therapist. I am there to represent the defendant and only him. I know everyone is afraid in this situation, but I also know that attorneys can't be the best advocates if we allow ourselves to become overwhelmed by the family's emotions.

In addition to the family's fears about what will happen to their boy if he is sucked into the system, we have to deal with their internalization of the mistakes the boy has just made. *Why did this happen? What did I do wrong? Was I a bad parent? Was I too lenient? Too strict?*

All of this inner turmoil is heaped upon the attorney. A lot of my clients tend to be young, low- to middle-income black males who have gotten into serious trouble for the first time. The boys who are middle income typically weren't lacking in resources and opportunities growing up; many were fortunate enough to have a father in the home. So you can imagine the questions swirling around in their parents' heads, the self-doubt gnawing away at them.

But we attorneys have to sit there, listening to their anguish and dismay, and divorce ourselves from the emotions with which the family is dealing in order to do our jobs. This is a skill that all attorneys develop over time. Early in my career, I wasn't as good at divorcing myself emotionally, and I would let a family's trauma overwhelm me, drain me, and render me less effective as defense counsel.

I have learned to establish early in my first meeting with the client and the family that I will not be the mother confessor. While I am sympathetic to their struggles, I cannot be called upon to heal the family's pain.

I say all of this right away. They nod in understanding—and then most of them proceed to dump all of their stuff on me anyway.

It is wise for families to try to avoid using the attorney as a whipping post or mother/father confessor. Permit them the freedom to defend your loved one properly, without the weight of your guilt, pain, and recrimination. You have placed your trust in a professional, so permit that professional to go to work on behalf of your loved one.

The modern apparatus of the public defender evolved in the wake of the 1963 US Supreme Court decision in *Gideon vs. Wainwright*, which established that state courts are required under the Fourteenth Amendment to provide lawyers in criminal cases to represent defendants who can't afford their own attorneys. But in the day-to-day reality of the criminal justice system, this lofty standard set by the Supreme Court is seldom realized in most states. The result is that many indigent clients receive inadequate counsel. Thousands of Americans are shipped off to jail every year because the nation doesn't care enough about their fate to make sure the system abides by its own rules.

While there are many extremely able attorneys working as public defenders, it is nearly impossible for them to give each case the attention it deserves, because in many places they have caseloads that could easily soar into the hundreds. According to the National Legal Aid & Defender Association, while national standards aim to limit felony caseloads to 150 per year per attorney, it is more common for public defenders to have annual caseloads of 500, 600, 800, or more. A *New York Times* investigation found defenders with caseloads of more than 1,600 a year. A load like that means many don't even have time to talk to their clients before making a hurried guilty plea once the prosecutor makes the plea offer.

It is not humanly possible for any attorney to investigate, draft motions, argue motions, do legal research, interview witnesses, and prepare a file for trial if her caseload is that extreme.

Luckily, between the public defender's office and the high-profile attorneys whose names fill newspaper headlines because of their high-profile clients, there's a vast network of attorneys available who can provide excellent counsel in your time of need. They are not cheap, but they won't necessarily require you to take out a second mortgage on your house to pay for their services.

For every Mark O'Mara in Florida or Bruce Harvey in Georgia, with rates that can soar well beyond $400 an hour, there's a host of equally talented lawyers who will likewise exert every effort to ensure that the system operates properly and every client receives a fair shot at justice.

We were all raised hearing our parents admonish, "Don't call me from a jail cell." Most parents actually see their children reach adulthood without receiving that call. Unfortunately, many others hear that shrill ring from the jail. But rather than harkening back to that admonition, we need to ensure that our children receive adequate support during a crisis.

The truth is, every single day Americans are accused of crimes they didn't commit, or severely overcharged for an offense they may have committed, or are the victims of an egregious range of other mistakes that occur in the criminal justice process. In all of these instances, walking into the police station with a "once you're arrested, I'm washing my hands of you" attitude would do an enormous disservice to one's child and to the preparation of an adequate defense.

Everyone has heard horror stories about the failures of public defenders. While you're sitting in church, or working out at the gym, or in line at the grocery store, you've likely overheard someone recounting the tale of a relative who was railroaded because the public defender didn't do his job properly. Or you might have had such a story in your own family.

My problems with the public defender system are mainly focused on their caseload, not their competency. I have seen many skilled attorneys toiling away as public defenders. But their main enemy is time. They just don't have enough hours in the day.

But the truth is that any attorney—whether a public defender or not—might not be doing the best job for you. Fortunately, there are many ways that a client can tell whether his attorney is providing him a rigorous defense:

1. Are your phone calls returned? I think this is by far the biggest complaint I hear about defense attorneys—that they never return their clients' calls. I must admit that I am sometimes guilty of this, taking too long to get back to a client who has reached out to me. In my younger days, when in some years I had as many as 100 major felony criminal cases throughout the year, with many of them going to trial, I was particularly bad with this kind of client contact. I'd talk to my clients when we got close to needing to appear in court or file something in their case—in other words, when I needed them, not when they needed me. I was literally running from courtroom to courtroom, jail to jail, talking to clients, moving along their files. Any phone calls were going to have to be returned by my assistant. Even though I always gave my speech about me representing the client and not the family early on, the family would still call with a million questions.

I have learned that I am a better attorney when my caseload is much lower. So over the years, I have become more discriminating when choosing cases, which allows me to spend more time on each individual file and return my clients' calls in a more timely fashion.

But I must say that whether your attorney is a public defender or in private practice, she is very likely an extremely busy individual who doesn't have enough hours in the day to do everything she needs to do. Understanding that, don't let unreturned phone calls be the *only* criteria you use in evaluating her competency.

2. Are motions being filed? Whether they challenge statements you made to police, or the legality of the police stop or search of the vehicle, or the testimony of an eyewitness, there are *always* motions that can be filed on your behalf. If your attorney hasn't filed any motions and hasn't challenged anything coming from the prosecutor, you need to find out why.

3. Have you been asked personal questions about yourself? This is especially relevant when you are being represented by a public defender. Soon after the attorney has been retained, she should question you thoroughly to learn your background and get a sense of you. She should want to know what your story is, how you were raised, and your educational background. An attorney never knows where an incredibly relevant piece of information that may seem minor and innocuous to you or your family members might be buried. So she has to dig to see what's there. I don't know how one can practice law without having crucial information about a client's background, but I've seen it done.

If the only questions you have gotten involve your name, your address, and a telephone number for next of kin, you might be in trouble. You don't want the first contact from your attorney to be when she gets a plea offer from the state and she's looking at you and telling you to plead guilty. But it happens all the time, particularly in drug cases. Say you're facing a felony drug charge, a first offense, and without even sending any discovery to your defense counsel, the state is offering you five years probation as a first offender. In Georgia, that means you don't even have to admit guilt. If you successfully complete five years on probation, you won't have a criminal record. That's incredibly enticing. You get to go home, the prosecutor disposes of a case, and the defense attorney considers her job done and never bothers to look any further.

But the problem is, too many young people tend to get in trouble again. Despite their promises to the court and their family members and everybody else they can make promises to, they somehow find a way during that five years to violate the terms of their probation. When that happens, their first-offender status gets revoked, the conviction gets placed on their record, and they might have to spend some time in prison. All the while, if that defense attorney had bothered to ask for the discovery and taken a look at the state's initial case, she might have seen that, say, the

Terry stop that secured the evidence in the first place was totally illegal and likely would have been thrown out by the court—meaning the client would have walked away without a conviction, let
alone any probation.

4. Isn't it too late to hire a new attorney after a plea has already been
offered? Though prosecutors sometimes try to make it appear as
if you have just minutes to decide on a plea—and though I have
seen judges try to push defendants to take a plea—in most cases,
if you tell the court you and your family want to hire another
attorney to represent you, the judge will continue the case to a
later date. A judge can't force you to take a plea. The judge will
say you and your new attorney need to be in court by a certain
date, maybe a month or so into the future. If you don't have a new
attorney by that date, the court will conclude that you are playing games—perhaps thinking that in time, the prosecution will
reduce the plea offer. The court will not look favorably upon such
delaying tactics, so you must find an attorney as soon as you can.
When your folks come to see you, you must impress upon them
the gravity of the situation, telling them your attorney has done
nothing on your behalf or that it doesn't seem as if the attorney
has looked at the discovery. In these cases, it's incumbent upon
your family to somehow find someone else to represent you.

I was recently able to get charges dismissed against a client
whose family came to me in desperation, telling me that their
child's attorney had never even talked to him about the case until
the prosecutor came with a plea offer—an offer that included
time in prison.

But I also had a client whose family told him not to cooperate
with me because, at the time, I was in the role of court-appointed
attorney. The family had heard all the horror stories about public
defenders and believed from the outset that there was no way I
could be competent. They were trying to hire their own attorney

to represent the young man, so they inexplicably told him not to cooperate with me, the court-appointed counsel.

I can't think of any circumstances in which it is a good idea to withhold information from your attorney. My client had been charged with murder. Time passed. We were scheduled for trial, my client's family still hadn't hired an attorney, and my client still refused to talk to me. Due to my court-appointed status, I couldn't withdraw. I tried to withdraw, telling the judge that my client refused to cooperate with me, but as I had expected, the judge wouldn't let me out. He instead admonished my client to cooperate with me so that I could prepare a defense.

At the eleventh hour, the family finally found an attorney to take over the case. I have never been so happy to turn over a case file; I was hopeful that the client would now feel comfortable co-operating with his new attorney. Ultimately, however, the young man was convicted of murder. In the early stages of the case, the state had produced no evidence that placed him at the scene of the crime. The murder victim had been shot through a door and, while the co-defendant said my client was the one who fired the shot, the state had no proof. You can't convict someone solely on the statement of a co-conspirator. But the state found a latent print that placed the client at the scene of the crime. And that was it; this young man was convicted of the murder and got a sentence somewhere in the neighborhood of 130 years in prison. The young man was just 19, so in effect he will spend the rest of his life in prison. Of course, there was also a shooting victim, who tragically was killed; whether this young man did the crime or not, two lives essentially were thrown away.

At some later point, I actually ran into this young man in jail. I was there talking to another client who had recently taken a plea and my former client was in the same pod. He apologized to me and said, "I know that you were trying. And I heard you're a really good attorney. I'm sorry I didn't talk to you." This broke my heart.

Ultimately it's not about me, it's about the client. Talking to me might have resulted in a plea deal with less time in prison.

Whether you are being represented by a public defender or a private attorney, there are still things you can do to help your case and maximize your chances of going home.

The most important question to remember is the following:

5. Have you told your attorney everything? I can't stress enough the magnitude of this piece of advice. It may seem obvious, but clients and their families ignore it all the time. Every tiny bit of information needs to be passed on to your attorney, even things that seem irrelevant or inconsequential. Naturally, you want to give your attorney contact information for any person who can corroborate where you were on the night in question and what you were doing. This means not just your homies, but also maybe the bouncer at the club who nodded to you on the way in, or the bartender who slid you a drink, or the waitress who took your order.

In addition, you must provide every shred of information about your background. Were you abused as a child? Did you experience some sort of deprivation? Were you in special education because of a learning disability or psychological or emotional problems? Many young people who go on to commit crimes have a history of some sort of developmental or psychological disorder that might prove relevant to the defense. Others might have disorders that have been undiagnosed, but which were expressed through early signs. If your lawyer is aware of some of these issues, she might be able to get you diagnosed, which could greatly help your case.

Divulging such personal and potentially embarrassing information isn't always easy for defendants and their families. But after nearly two decades in practice, I can spot things. I see the signs, and put together the indicators. Maybe they were underachievers in school who barely squeaked through or dropped out. I start probing, asking the mother questions, and finally she might say something like, "Well, we didn't want to get him tested."

I understand that a lot of black people fear labels and thus are leery of having their children diagnosed with learning disabilities, but if you know something is wrong, you do that child a disservice if you don't investigate the problem. I'm not trying to pivot into playing a social worker here, but I will say from an attorney's standpoint that if a child has underlying problems that impede his learning and development, you've done him no favors by avoiding a label and thus refusing to have him treated. If his school is pushing you to have him evaluated, bring the child to a private psychologist first to avoid an automatic placement that might be triggered by the system's psychologists. Treatment and medication can save young people from a lifetime of despair. It's always better to know than to stick your head in the sand. Studies show that a good education is the most surefire way to keep young people away from criminal activity.

When the court appoints a private attorney to represent you, you don't have any control over which attorney you get. It's the luck of the draw. In the early days of my practice, I would sometimes get clients through contracts with the court on a county-by-county basis, but in 2003, the state enacted the Georgia Indigent Defense Act, which created a statewide agency to ensure that indigent defendants get adequate representation. One of the major roles of this agency, the Georgia Public Defender Standards Council, is to appoint counsel in cases that have multiple defendants. For instance, many armed robbery cases in the Atlanta metro area are alleged to have been committed by groups of individuals. Since each defendant has to be represented by a different office, the GPDSC has to retain counsel for each defendant.

I had a case several years ago where my client, who I'll call "Ricky," was alleged to have been part of a group of a dozen or so kids who went on a gay-bashing and armed-robbery rampage in Atlanta's Piedmont Park, the bucolic centerpiece of the city. About seven of them were charged, meaning the court needed to appoint separate attorneys for each of them. Ricky was the youngest of the group, and I was able to get his charges transferred to juvenile court.

At times, people become confused about how the system works. By word-of-mouth, they'll hear about favorable verdicts I was able to get in some court-appointed cases, and they'll come to me wanting the same outcome for free, like I did for their friend.

This brings us to an essential question:

6. *How do you find an attorney?* I believe word-of-mouth will always be the best method of finding an attorney. Start asking around, and it won't take long to find someone willing to share information about a positive experience with an attorney. If the defendant is under the age of 26 or so, the parents usually hire the attorney. Try asking family members, friends, or colleagues. Nearly all of my retained cases come to me through referrals from past clients.

There are also quite a few websites where you can find listings of lawyers, such as martindale.com, avvo.com, and justia.com. Do you have concerns about an attorney you find through one of these general resources? You can check with your state's bar association to find out if a particular attorney has been the subject of any disciplinary actions.

Often an initial meeting will be with the entire family, so it's important that everyone is clear that even if the parents are footing the bill, the attorney is being hired to represent the client. That means the attorney can't discuss the particulars of the case with other family members. When an attorney has discussions with a parent or sibling, those discussions are for a limited purpose. Discussions with family members are not protected by the attorney-client privilege; if substantive issues are discussed and overheard, those matters are not protected in court. This may seem like a minor point, but if a crucial piece of information was passed on to me through a family member and it somehow leaked out to the opposition, we could be forced to reveal the entire contents of our conversation to the court.

If the young person has not been locked up, I will meet with him in my office to start collecting the background information I need. If he is behind bars, then I'll have to visit him in jail to begin my discussions with him.

As I said before, there are a slew of skilled attorneys out there who may not have their names in the newspapers every week. It is often said that the rich can buy not-guilty verdicts—that having the funds to hire an expensive lawyer will yield you better results. In reality, I think the matter is a bit more complicated. In the final analysis, the facts of the case will be the most important factor in determining the outcome. If you have bad facts, no dollar amount is going to buy you the verdict you want. But it's like a medical procedure: You are always going to want the best surgeon and the best facility to perform the procedure.

7. How much is a good attorney going to cost me? It varies by attorney and is dependent on the nature of the offense, but I think for a common crime like an armed robbery, you're likely going to have to pay an attorney a retainer somewhere in the neighborhood of $10,000. That's the down payment; the costs go up from there. Some attorneys bill hourly, working off that retainer as they bill you by the hour. When the money runs out, you will get a bill for the remainder as they continue to work.

I'm a flat-fee attorney. What that means is I've used my years of experience to calculate in my head how much of my time and brainpower it's going to take to handle your case, then I quote you a flat fee to cover my advocacy. Mind you, if I have to hire investigators or experts to help the client, their fees must be paid on top of mine. While some attorneys require you to pay a portion up front with a retainer, I allow my clients to pay their bill on a payment plan, acknowledging the realities of today's economic environment. I understand that most families will not be able to get their hands on $20,000 or $30,000 in one fell swoop. Many other highly skilled and qualified attorneys will similarly allow you to make payments, with the final installment due before a final plea or trial calendar.

Let me also say something else on behalf of public defenders. When they have the time to devote to cases, some of them can be extremely effective, because they've seen everything under the sun. Many private attorneys may not have seen as many armed robbery cases as a public defender has. So while the high-priced attorney can assign young associates to do the research needed, he or she might not have top-of-mind access to the ins and outs of defending an armed robbery. The more you see it, the more you understand it. The more you understand it, the better you're able to plot out certain fact patterns. When I was handling 100 cases a year, the majority of them were armed robberies, many of them multi-defendant crimes. Almost instantly, I could identify the cases that were likely to be more successful at trial versus those where the defendant didn't have a prayer. So those kinds of calculations would be helpful when the prosecutor came bearing a plea offer.

But I must add that even when my gut tells me that my client is guilty as hell, it's still always been difficult for me to advise them to take the plea. It's part of my makeup to want to fight, to want to push the state to meet its burden. That fighting spirit, in my opinion, is what you want to find in an attorney.

Chapter 6: Get a Haircut

The Black Male Goes to Trial

JUST A GLIMPSE of the nightly television news in America leaves me drained and depressed. Like a mind-numbing parade of pathology, the brown faces flash across the screen, blurry mug shots capturing the rage and despair of black boys in the richest nation on earth.

When the crime is especially heinous or stupid, I hold my breath, like many African Americans, as the reporter breathlessly describes the scene, always making it sound like the most horrific act that's ever been committed. Through my mind dances the official black prayer: *Lord, please don't let it be a black man.*

But often it is.

Though I feel we are now seeing pictures of white defendants with growing regularity, it sometimes seems as if white people don't commit crimes—which we know is far from the truth.

As a defense attorney, I know how this black male parade looks to much of the outside world: African-American male = criminal.

So when I am called to represent a black male, one of my primary goals is to make sure my client looks as little as possible like the faces the jury sees in that nightly black-male-crime parade. If I fail, and if the members of my jury look over to my table and believe they see a criminal, my client is doomed. If they see a scared but earnest and honest young man, then we have a chance. I have to make him human to them—to make him look more like their own son or nephew than like those scary guys on the evening news.

Increasingly, a mane of long dreadlocks frames the black male faces on the nightly news. Locs have become the hairstyle of choice for a large swath of urban America—no doubt inspired by rappers like Lil Wayne and 2 Chainz, as well as a slew of professional athletes, particularly in the NFL. Aware of this trend, I now have to take the unfortunate step of making my clients cut off their locs so as to give them the best chance with a jury. I would say the same perception probably arises with hairstyles like braids and cornrows—anything that is immediately attached to urban America.

After getting rid of their hair issues, the next thing I look at is their dress, their fingernails—everything the jury will be able to see. I encourage them to get a manicure and buy a suit in an effort to look as clean-cut as possible. Many young males like to wear their nails long for various and sundry reasons. Many jury members will be aware that a long pinky fingernail might signify a drug user. So the long nails have got to go.

And then there are the tattoos. I'm aware that they have become a virtual must-have accessory among America's youth—after all, I have a teenage daughter—but it's undeniable that a body blanketed with tattoos doesn't give the jury the best impression of a young man. We can cover them up when they're splashed across the arms and some of the neck, but when they crawl above the collar and even on the face, there's not much that can be done except pray that we get a few tattoo aficionados on the jury.

I had a client named Charles who had tats all over his body, including on his cheek, his forehead, and his hands. Charles had been charged with the murder of a two-year-old girl, the daughter of one of his relatives, whom he and his girlfriend had volunteered to care for. His tattoos certainly didn't help his image. It may not have mattered—when we're talking about the death of a child, the jury wants someone to go to prison—but Charles was convicted.

When I first met a former client named Shawn, practically the first thing out of his mouth was his vehement assertion of his innocence. Shawn had been accused of armed robbery and he wanted me to believe that he didn't do it. But the first thing I noticed about him was his beautiful hair. His dreadlocks were meticulously well groomed, a gorgeous river of tight black coils that flowed down his back. He clearly had been growing them for at least a decade. Right away I knew he wouldn't be eager to cut them off.

Shawn was facing what's known in legal parlance as "bad facts." He and a friend had gone to visit a girl they knew. They were sitting around in her house, talking, not doing much, when another girl that Shawn had never met joined them. In addition to the four of them, there were also two young children in the house. Shawn stepped outside for a minute, telling them he was going to look for something in his car. But as he started to walk up the stairs to go back in the house, he saw a guy with a gun going into the house. So Shawn ran off to find somebody to call the police.

When Shawn saw the gunman leave the house, he ran back in to make sure the ladies were okay. The gunman had taken a flat-screen television, cellphones, other valuables in the house, plus cash from the second young lady, who had just gotten paid.

When Shawn walked in, the young lady who didn't know him started screaming and cursing, "You set us up to get robbed! You set us up!"

Stunned, Shawn and his friend decided to leave. When they got down to his car, they were greeted by the gunman and another guy. The gunman said, "Drive." The gunman and his accomplice got in the backseat while Shawn and his friend got in the front. It was dusk, and Shawn pulled away without turning on his headlights. Just then, the police showed up on the block and the police car headed straight at them.

"Stop!" the police yelled.

When the car stopped, the two guys in the backseat got out and started running. The police found the gun underneath the rear tire, where the gunman had placed it right after he got out of the car. Things got even worse for them: the police found the flat-screen TV in the trunk of Shawn's car.

This was my first trial in years, as I had been working as in-house counsel in corporate America for quite a few years prior. I somehow had to get the jury to believe that my client and his friend didn't have anything to do with the armed robbery—even though they were driving away with the other two guys in the car, the gun was found by the back wheel, and the flat-screen TV was in the trunk. How could the bad guys possibly get the flat-screen TV in the trunk without the assistance of the person with the keys to the trunk? If I couldn't believably answer that question, my client would be going to jail.

Shawn was the sweetest kid in the world, and his family was extremely supportive. Everybody in his family was calling me about the case—his grandfather, his uncle, his cousins, his mother. His father was deceased, but he had a tremendous family network, which was unusual among such clients. Not all families are as invested in the success of a case that involves one of their young loved ones. As difficult as it may be to believe, some families completely disappear when a child gets in trouble. It was Shawn's first offense, and the state had offered five years of incarceration, which was half of the ten years it would customarily offer for armed robberies. The state couldn't prove Shawn ever had a gun in his hand, which I believe is what brought the offer down to five years. But Shawn's family kept insisting that Shawn shouldn't go to prison for something he didn't do—though there were a few relatives urging him to take the offer, since he was facing in the neighborhood of 80–100 years in prison if convicted at trial. At bottom, Shawn was looking at going away for the rest of his life.

The closer we got to trial, the more I impressed upon Shawn the need to cut his hair. Finally, one day I sat him down and had a heart-to-heart. I explained to him that 90 percent of the people we now see on the nightly news accused of committing crimes are wearing their hair in dreadlocks and running around with their pants sagging below their butts. I told him his task was to present himself to the jury as someone who is completely different from the guys they see on the news.

On the first day of jury selection, Shawn walked into the courthouse with his mom and his uncles—and he had cut his hair. The locs were gone and he was wearing a black jacket, black pants, and a crisp white shirt. I was so proud of him. It was exactly how I needed him to look.

When a client has the money to pay, attorneys sometimes hire expensive jury consultants to help them pick the jury members. My clients rarely have the money to afford consultants, so usually it's just me. But over the years, I have picked juries so many times that I am now at that place where I know I can trust my gut. There's a lot of psychology at work in jury selection; the topic is frequently covered in continuing legal education seminars, because lawyers spend a lot of time thinking and talking about trial preparation and strategy. You learn to read body language, such as understanding what it means when someone crosses her arms while you're talking, or if he nods a lot when you make points. With black male defendants, I need a jury that will be receptive to them and open-minded about the case we're going to present. They can't be thinking about the guys they saw on the nightly news.

But even before we get to their perceptions of my clients, the first challenge is getting them to like me as the attorney. You know in the movie *Jerry Maguire* when Renee Zellweger says to Tom Cruise, "You had me at hello"? Well, an attorney has to get the jury to like her at hello, too. The way I dress, the way I speak, the way I take command of the courtroom, whether the jurors look me in the eye—these all are indicators of the way the jury will respond to me, and thus to my client. I have to look at the jury members in such a way that I am conveying to them the message that I know they are an important part of this process, that I appreciate them, and that I understand that they are human beings worthy of my spending time trying to get to know them. It's all a very delicate, important dance.

There's always a considerable amount of attention paid to a jury's racial makeup. When a case is "high profile," attracting lots of media attention, that's one of the first pieces of information the reporter will put in the story. Sometimes it's the *only* piece of information about the jury that gets reported. Certainly, when your client is African American, you would prefer as many African Americans on your jury as possible. But sometimes you can't get what you want. I had a trial in Fayette County where the jury pool I was presented with didn't even come close to reflecting the current racial makeup of the county. I was incensed. The county had not updated the jury pool in well over a decade, so the people being called in for jury duty were overwhelmingly white—in a county where one out of every five residents is now black. We had two days of grueling hearings over this issue. I still ended up with a predominantly white jury for the case, but I also got a pleasant surprise after the trial: two jurors, an older white female and an older white male, both of whom were staunch Republicans, came up to me after the trial to tell me they felt bad for my client, a young black male, because they didn't believe the alleged teenage female robbery victim.

"You were the best attorney in the entire courtroom," the man said to me.

I was taken aback, and once again learned a lesson about juries that attorneys learn over and over: you can't predict what a jury will do, and you can't predict how a particular juror will respond to you and your client. While I was afraid of those predominantly white jurors, they were trying to wrestle with how to give my client a break. Just because jurors are white, I can't assume they will be our enemy.

On the flip side, I can't make any assumptions about what a black juror will do either. In that same Fayette County case, the main juror who persuaded the others toward guilt was a black male. The man had six daughters, and when he looked at my client, I believe he was thinking about those daughters. I put him on the jury because he was the only black male in the pool. But it was a mistake; I should have given more weight to all those daughters.

Juries pay close attention to the relationship between attorneys and our clients.

I see them watching us constantly. When I walked into the courtroom with Shawn—his locs now gone and wearing his shiny new suit—I knew the eyes of the jury members would be on us from start to finish. If an attorney sits there next to the client and never interacts with him, never touches him, never makes eye contact, the jury is going to get the impression that the attorney doesn't like the client. That's going to be a problem for the client during jury deliberations.

I encourage defendants to consider showing affection—or, failing that, at least a sense of regard and connection—to their attorneys during a trial. I let my client know that I will put my arm around him; I will pull on him to get his attention; I will whisper things in his ear. I will even scold him if he's giving too much of a reaction to something. The entire effect, I believe, is one of a mother protecting her child. In my experience, juries like to see that; I think it makes the client appear more human, more vulnerable. While female attorneys can take on the motherly role, male attorneys have other tools they can use with black male defendants that are helpful, such as appearing to be a father figure who can control and teach the boy.

Let me say that my affection is usually not an act I'm putting on. By the time I get to trial with the huge majority of my clients, I have developed a real affection for them. I know their families. I know their struggles. I know their backgrounds. It's not hard to have affection for these boys. Though they may try to project this hard outer shell, so often I see right through it to the frightened and needy boy underneath the surface, looking for love and protection—two things that are in short supply for too many black boys in our society. I'm talking about males who might have been accused of murder or armed robbery or carjacking or a violent home invasion. In other words, to many people, the very epitome of the scary black man.

At the same time defense attorneys are trying to show their clients in the best possible light, as vulnerable and sympathetic, prosecutors will be working hard to send the jury as many signals as possible that these defendants are grown man to be feared. Though he wasn't the prosecutor, that's what Mark O'Mara was able to do in the George Zimmerman murder trial—make the jury believe that seventeen-year-old Trayvon Martin was one of those black males that you should fear. The jury let Zimmerman walk away.

It's also what the defense attorney was trying to do in the trial of Michael Dunn, who was charged with murdering seventeen-year-old Jordan Davis after Dunn got into an argument with Davis and his three friends about the loud music they were playing in their SUV. Dunn's attorney was able to convince enough jurors that Dunn feared for his life because he thought he saw a shotgun in the SUV (a shotgun the boys said doesn't exist)—and that he was justified in riddling the SUV with ten bullets, three of which hit Davis. The jury convicted Dunn of three counts of attempted murder for shooting into the SUV, but it curiously deadlocked on the murder charge. So some members of that twelve-member Florida jury—which contained two black women, an Asian-American woman, an Hispanic man, and eight whites—were able to hold Dunn responsible for wantonly firing into the car, but not for having three of the bullets find a target.

"We cannot protect our children because racism in America is not merely a belief system but a heritage, and the inability of black parents to protect their children is an ancient tradition," Ta-Nehisi Coates wrote for TheAtlantic.com website after the Dunn verdict. "I insist that the irrelevance of black life has been drilled into this country since its infancy, and shall not be extricated through the latest innovations in Negro Finishing School."

By the time a case gets to trial, after months of battling over pre-trial motions, the prosecutor and defense attorney have usually developed a serious dislike for one another. Though we're frequently battling, we usually maintain our distance before the trial. There's not much friendly contact. In fact, if the prosecutor is burning up your telephone, you know there's something wrong with the state's case against your client.

After I had Shawn clean up for his trial, I was surprised that the prosecutor never brought up his booking picture during the trial to illustrate how different he now looked. If I were the prosecutor, I would have shown the jury a shot of his booking picture, with the locs, and noted that he had cut them off for some reason. But thankfully the prosecutor never thought to go there.

In the end, despite the extremely bad facts we were facing, the jury came back with a verdict of not guilty. Shawn was able to go home with his family. I was able to breathe a sigh of relief.

Young black males may not realize how frightening they can seem to others, and need to accept the advice of their counsel about how to shine a light on the person inside. It broke my heart when I read the story of Brian Banks, the high school football star in southern California who spent five years in jail, and another five years on probation, after being convicted of rape—only to have his accuser admit a decade later that she had made it all up. Banks was just sixteen when the girl accused him—hours after a kissing session—of rape and kidnapping.

While much of the media attention surrounding Banks focused on his attempts to make an NFL team after going a decade without playing football, I was disheartened to learn what Banks said about the circumstances that led to his jail time. Banks sat in a cell for a year, desperately awaiting the start of his trial, when the attorney his mother had hired (she sold her house and car to pay for the attorney's services) would get a chance to put his accuser on the stand and tear apart her fabricated story. But just before Banks was about to enter the courtroom, he got a visit in the holding tank from his attorney, who told him that she had gotten an "amazing" plea offer from the district attorney. He could plead no contest to one count of rape and receive a likely sentence of probation from the judge. Banks said his lawyer told him, "I can tell you right now, this will be an all-white jury, and as soon as you walk into that courtroom, a big black teenager, they will see you as guilty."

Facing the possibility of 41 years in prison if convicted, Banks took the deal—particularly since his attorney had promised him he would likely get probation. But then the judge shocked everybody by giving him the maximum of six years in prison. Banks, still just seventeen, was shuttled off to a cell and never got to face his accuser.

It's horrific that a black boy would be told to take a plea just because he's big and black. What a damning statement that is about the stigma of being black and male in America. After all, it's the attorney's job to figure out how to humanize him to the jury. Banks seems to be an attractive, well-spoken young man— but even if he was big, black, and scary-looking, he's still a human being and he still has a human story to tell. Assuming Banks' story of his plea is true, then this is racial profiling at its worst, where your own attorney denies you your constitutional right because you're a "big, black" male.

In summary, I need every person reading this chapter to understand that a defendant and his attorney must do everything in their power to present the best possible case to the jury. This is not the time to make a sociological statement about the perception of black males in our society, or to refuse to make any changes because you think the world needs to accept you as you are. There are times and places to make those kinds of political stands—a criminal trial is not a good time or place. Instead, you have to concern yourself with the question of how you will be perceived by your potential jury—whether that jury is all white, all black, or somewhere in between—and work to put your best foot forward. If you do not, the consequences for you will be extremely dire.

You and your attorney should go through the following checklist:

- Hair as clean cut as possible
- Fingernails clean and well manicured
- Tattoos as invisible as possible
- Clothes clean and conservative—a dark suit is well advised
- Face and demeanor as warm and welcoming as possible—this means lose the scowl
- Body language as friendly and nonthreatening as you can manage, particularly toward your attorney

Chapter 7: Jesus...Somebody...Please Help!

Never Give Up Hope

I DIDN'T DO IT.

Perhaps there is no refrain that defense attorneys hear from clients more than that one. In fact, this refrain is so common that an attorney might be tempted to dismiss it. After all, defense lawyers are in the business of reasonable doubt, not guilt. Isn't that the lesson we got from Mark O'Mara, George Zimmerman's attorney in the Trayvon Martin case?

But sometimes, the words are actually true.

There are occasions when we lawyers know deep down in our bones that our client has been railroaded. These are the cases that keep defense attorneys up at night, our thoughts burdened with worry, our fears pushing us to use every resource, every tool in our box, to get our client out of the jaws of the system.

Indeed, these are the cases that belie the wisdom of the plea bargain—that demonstrate how difficult it can be for young black males to make it to adulthood without becoming ensnared in a system programmed to believe in their guilt at every turn.

These are cases that sometimes seem impossible to win, especially when there is a mountain of bad facts stacked against the client—cases that make attorneys want to summon a higher authority for assistance. To my utter joy, on many occasions my prayers have been answered. Something completely unexpected has dropped into my lap and lit a path to freedom for my client. Sometimes even the most daunting circumstances can shift in an instant.

The message here is simple: *Never give up hope.*

As an example, I'll never forget the case of Phillip White. Phillip had a friend who was suspected in a murder case and the detectives knew this friend had not acted alone. When a detective called Phillip and his father to come in and discuss the case, they felt no qualms about going down to the station to talk to the detective without consulting a lawyer. Turns out that wasn't such a good idea. After the detective assured them that Phillip wouldn't run into any trouble, because he wasn't involved, the district attorney's office decided to go ahead and charge Phillip as an accessory—a course decided on in part due some of the statements Phillip made to the detective.

By the time I was brought on to the case, a full two years later, the state had accumulated a mountain of evidence against Phillip, including an eyewitness statement from a surviving witness—the sister of the murder victim—putting Phillip at the scene of the murder. Phillip had an alibi: His girlfriend's brother had been killed around the time of the alleged murder, and Phillip had been with the girl and her family the entire time. But the prosecution still had this witness, putting him at the scene.

Phillip's family was anxious and troubled, calling me constantly, letting me know that Phillip, who had been in jail for nearly two years, *had* to be exonerated. When I visited Phillip, I asked him to help me figure out what had happened, how we had gotten to this point, but he had no idea. He just kept telling me, *I didn't have anything to do with it.* I was stumped. I knew Phillip wasn't going to present the most appealing figure to the jury—he was a scrawny kid who clearly hadn't had the easiest life. He had a long goatee and wore those long, drug-user pinkie fingernails.

I knew I couldn't clean him up enough for him to fit the well-scrubbed image of the innocent young American male. I was out of options. The only thing left was for me to ask Jesus for help.

Then I sat down with the eyewitness—the sister of the murder victim—to interview her a month before we were to go to trial. Little things had started to bubble up that made me want to dig further. The sister's description of the murderer didn't seem to match my client. Accompanied by my investigator, I knocked on the girl's front door. We talked to her mother and her cousin and then asked if she was home.

"Yeah, we'll go get her," they told us.

When she came in and sat down, she clearly had no idea who we were. She didn't know I was working for the man accused of murdering her sister. I showed her a picture of Phillip.

"Do you know who this is?"

She shook her head. "I don't know him," she said.

I was excited. Was this a break in the case?

I told the prosecutor what had transpired. He said he would look into it, but he didn't act until a week before the trial was supposed to start. When he met with the victim's sister, she cussed him out.

"I told y'all that wasn't him!" she said to them, referring to Phillip. "I don't know who the hell he is."

So the Friday before we were to begin jury selection on the following Monday, I got a call from the prosecutor telling me he was not going to proceed with charges against my client. Phillip was free to go. I was certain it was the result not just of good lawyering but also of intervention from on high—a prime example of the need to always keep the faith.

I recently read a study that said the brains of teenagers aren't fully formed until much later, so they are liable to engage in all manner of stupidity all the way up to the age of 27. Let me say I can enthusiastically endorse those study results just based on what I've seen in my practice over the years. I've had cases that left me shaking my head, wondering, *What the hell were you thinking?*

But for the sake of full disclosure, I must add that my friends and I were also capable of doing some incredibly dumb stuff when we were teenagers more than three decades ago. Thinking back on it now almost makes me want to blush. But we were living in different times, when the consequences of our idiocy didn't seem to be quite so severe.

The fact is that these days, more than ever, more and more youthful conduct is criminalized, with police aggressively patrolling the streets, looking for young people engaged in bad behavior, as I've said before. What young person back then didn't sometimes stumble into something silly and stupid? Maybe they shoplifted from the candy store, or spray-painted their names on a wall somewhere, or threw rocks or eggs at passing cars. A few decades ago, a cop might have let us go with a stern warning, or brought us home to face the wrath of our parents. Today, such behavior will get you locked up in the blink of an eye.

The criminal-justice system today works almost as though we should expect teens to behave as if they have the brains of adults—and to understand that if they don't, they could face criminal charges. How do you convey that idea to a 14-year-old boy? How can you get him to wrap his head around the idea that the fun prank he is cooking up with his homeboy could result in arrest and heartache? Just because the consequences are more severe now doesn't mean that teenaged boys and girls aren't going to keep doing the same kinds of stupid stuff they've always done.

In these kinds of circumstances, sometimes hope means we have to deal with a system that feels so punitive.

I had a client named James whose teenage libido led him into the grip of trouble that wasn't just bad, but profoundly frightening. One minute he was thinking about hooking up with some girls; the next minute he was an accessory to murder.

From a defense attorney's perspective, you couldn't get much more perfect than James: He was a high-school football star with decent grades and strong recommendations, and he was looking forward to going to college. He had dedicated himself to becoming something that didn't involve prison.

One night James got a call from a friend, someone he had met through his older brother. The friend said a few words that would melt any high-school boy's heart: "Hey man, let's go hang out with these college girls I know." James had a girlfriend at the time, but we're talking about college girls here. And better yet, they were college girls willing to spend some time with high school boys. James' friend was a bit older and had dropped out of high school, but he still liked to hang around the high school.

James changed into his fresh summer whites, eager to meet up with the young ladies, maybe go to the movies, see what happened from there. But shortly after James arrived at another friend's house with this older guy and a few other males, he began to feel like something wasn't quite right. The older guy kept insisting that they not leave until they were joined by another guy who James didn't know very well. But when the new guy showed up, the older guy who had invited James suddenly had to leave, claiming he had to go get his mom. He left, and then the rest of the guys wanted James to ride with them to another place where a different guy was going to meet them. It was all feeling bizarre to James, but with the lure of the college girls waiting at the end of the odyssey, James was still down for whatever.

The group headed out, under the guise of meeting the girls, but suddenly they took a detour. The next thing James knew, they were standing in the back of an abandoned subdivision and one of James' acquaintances stepped to the new guy. His nightmare was about to begin.

"Man, give me the cards!" he said to the new guy.

*What the f*ck are they talking about?* James asked himself. He had no idea what was going on. He was still waiting for the college girls. But then things got real bad in a hurry. James' acquaintance pulled out a gun.

*Oh sh*t!* James thought.

"Give me the cards!" the gunman demanded once again, this time pointing the gun at the new guy.

"Do what you need to do! I ain't giving you sh*t!" the new guy said.

So James' acquaintance raised the gun and pulled the trigger. *Boom!*

The new guy fell to the ground. James was stunned, thinking, *How did I get here?*

They made the new guy get in the trunk of the car, blood flowing from his gunshot wound. Within minutes, James' older friend—the one he had known all his life, who had been a friend to his brother, who used to pick him up sometimes from football practice as a favor to James' brother—showed up again and they drove the car to a park. At the park, they shot the new guy again. They left his body lying there and got back in the car. Then they started talking to James, this time using the language of fear and intimidation.

"Be cool, man, just be cool," they said to James.

"We know where you live," they said.

"We know you're cool with your mom," they said.

James perceived those words to be a threat. They drove to a gas station and told James they needed him to go inside and buy some gasoline. He did as he was told, his heart pounding in his chest the whole time. Whatever their plans were at this point, James knew he had to get away from them.

"I don't give a damn what y'all do, I need to go," he said. "Shoot me if you have to."

They let James out of the car. Once they pulled away, James later learned, the group went back to the park and set the dead guy's body on fire with the gasoline James had purchased.

It didn't take long for the police to show up at James' house. He was arrested and charged with arson and concealment of the death of another. When James got to the police station, he was distraught. He was begging the cops to make sure his mom was safe because of the threats the other guys had made.

When I was brought onto this case and got the chance to spend time and listen to James, I was taken by his earnestness. But he was facing an extremely difficult fact pattern. He admitted buying gasoline that had been used to torch another man's body. He admitted to police that he was in the car. But he kept saying he wasn't involved in the murder. I couldn't imagine how I could beat these charges at trial. The jury would be sitting there seeing that this other young man had been so cruelly killed, burned by gasoline my client admitted purchasing, and they would want to punish someone for that young man's death. When I talked to my attorney colleagues about the case and told them the fact pattern, they all said, "He's lying. He's leaving something out. There's no way they would take someone with them to commit a murder who would then be able to identify them."

But something about James' spirit was whispering in my ear that he was telling the truth. Of course attorneys hear their clients say, "I didn't do it" all the time. That's not unusual. I can't even say what it was that separated James from all the others. There was just something about him and his story that spoke to me. He was always able to look me in the eye when he told it and his voice was so brimming with emotion, and he was still, two years later, so very afraid for his family. This fear was so strong that the family moved to a different county.

I tried to appeal to the prosecutor, telling him my client was not involved. I was advocating for a plea where James would be able to attain first-offender status and not have to go to prison. But the prosecutor wanted him to spend some time in prison. At one point, I ran into the prosecutor in a hallway and again made my appeal.

"But who brings somebody with them who will be a witness and them not be involved?" the prosecutor asked. "I've seen a lot of these cases. This is what I usually do. Not to burn your boy, but he's gotta be involved."

"But what if you're wrong?" I said. "What if this time, your guess is wrong? How are you going to be able to live with yourself, knowing the opportunities this kid had that were cut short because he wound up having to go to prison for something he wasn't involved in?"

"But what if *you're* wrong?" he said back to me.

To make matters worse, one of the co-defendants was taking a blind plea, which is what happens when the state and the defense don't agree on what the plea should be. He was taking a blind plea under the guise of giving testimony against my client and against the shooter. It was looking really bad for James. I had no idea how I was going to extricate him.

But then something happened. The prosecution came across a recording of James when he made his first statement to police. On the recording, he was literally hysterical, afraid of the other guys, afraid that they would do something to his mother and his family.

"I'm going to help you guys, but you have to help me keep my family safe!" he told the cops.

The prosecutor and his assistant called me up and said they would like to meet with James and me. On the way to the meeting, I told him, "Don't say anything. Let me do the talking. We have to see what they're talking about."

We sat down across from them. And I couldn't believe what they said next.

"We believe your client," the prosecutor said. "Upon closer review of the file…"

He went on to explain the details, but the result was simple: They were dismissing the charges against James. He was walking free—after he testified in court against the other guys.

While James never played football again, he did extremely well in college. In fact he founded an on-campus group to work with other young black men to encourage fellowship, accountability, responsibility, and honesty. I'm so proud of his success.

James' experience offers a crucial lesson that all young people need to carry around with them: You have to be extra careful at all times about who you associate with. If your gut tells you a situation feels wrong, you have to trust your gut and get the hell out of there. *Run.* Otherwise you could easily find yourself in a predicament like James'—you know you're innocent, but from the outside your innocence looks extremely questionable and even harder to prove.

I see this stuff all the time: You're in your mom's car, driving around with some guys, maybe one or two are your friends, and there are a couple of guys in the car whom you don't know very well. All of a sudden, somebody decides he wants to go in the convenience store to buy a pack of gum or something equally insignificant. Next thing you know, he's running back to your mom's car, talking about, "Drive! Drive!" And you find out he just robbed the store—and the store had a camera that recorded your mom's license plate.

You just got yourself implicated in an armed robbery—and will soon be trying to explain to a lawyer like me that you had no idea what your "friends" were going to do in the store. Imagine the look on your mother's face when the police come knocking at her door. The thought of that look alone should be enough to make you wary about driving around with guys you don't know very well.

Chapter 8: Families

Got to Be There

FOR PARENTS OF ANY COLOR, prison looms as the ultimate symbol of perceived parenting failure. When your boy was an adorable baby crawling across the bed to plant a wet kiss on your face, you could never imagine that he might wind up in the jaws of the criminal justice system.

That's why parents and family members are typically so distraught and overwhelmed when they get that phone call from the police station after their boy has been arrested. It is surely one of the most upsetting and traumatic times in the life of any family.

But while parents inevitably react to a child's arrest with a mixture of anger, frustration, shame, and dismay, the one thing families need to remember in this time of crisis can be summed up in a simple, seven-letter word: Support.

This is the moment when a young person most needs the support of family members: when he is facing the unbending wrath—

and the insistent need for bodies—of the prison-industrial complex. And the best way for the family to offer that support is to consult with a lawyer before making *any* statements to the police or anybody else about the case in question.

Family members—mom, dad, grandparents, siblings, cousins—all need to understand that you don't *have* to talk to the police just because the police ask. You don't *have* to go down to the police station and make statements that can incriminate your child in a crime just because the police invite you down.

When called to the police station to talk to your child, your best response is some form of the following: *I prefer to do what's best for my child and get him an attorney. Let him know we'll be there to see him soon accompanied by his attorney.*

I understand that everyone parents differently. There are the hard-core parents who put a lock on the refrigerator door when their kid hits eighteen and do everything in their power to make sure that kid gets out of the house and heads to college, stopping just short of putting a sign on the front door: *It's time for you to go!* Or the fathers and mothers who bravely march their sons and (increasingly) their daughters down to the recruiting station and sign them up for the military on their eighteenth birthday, in order to get them off the streets and into a disciplined setting. Then there's the other extreme: parents who don't push their kids to get out of the house, who allow their kids a responsibility-free existence, letting them live in their rooms rent-free for years, and still paying for their phone bills, gas, and car insurance.

I don't pass judgment on any of these parenting styles. To each his or her own. But I do take issue with those parents who live by the vow that if the kid gets arrested, he's on his own—*I'm not going down to the jail to get you.* In the United States, someone is arrested every two seconds. There's a drug arrest every nineteen seconds. The clink of police handcuffs is the soundtrack of modern American society, as omnipresent as the sound of the blowing wind. It's all around us, everywhere we turn. As I hope I've proven in these pages, being arrested doesn't necessarily mean your child has committed a crime. And they don't stop being our children just because they've been arrested and charged with a crime.

We can take the approach of putting the lock on the refrigerator and pushing them out the front door, washing our hands, or we can continue to provide the love and care and support that most parents give their children throughout their lives. My child is still a teenager, but knowing how often I call and lean on my own mother for love and support, even now, it's clear to me that you never stop being a parent. So that love and support should include getting them adequate counsel if they get in trouble.

That support also must mean being smart. I've seen on too many occasions that, sometimes, our families unwittingly can be our worst enemies.

I had a kid who was arrested near his grandmother's house, in a different state than where the alleged crime occurred. When his grandmother arrived at the scene of the arrest, she asked an officer for permission to talk to him. The officer said yes, but stayed near the defendant. The conversation went as follows:

Grandmother: "Did you commit this murder?"

Grandson: "Yeah, but I didn't mean to do it."

The officer overheard the admission of guilt and testified to the conversation and its contents at the defendant's trial. I understand she was probably an old-school grandma, but when the criminal-justice system is already involved, family members have to resist trying to satisfy their own sense of I-know-I-raised-this-boy-right-and-he's-going-to-tell-me-the-truth justice. We have to temper that with the knowledge that this child is being taken into custody and *anything* that's said can be used against him—anything from his mouth and anything from anybody else's mouth.

We also have to understand that when the police are reaching out to the family, they are not just contacting you out of the blue. There's a reason for it.

I have a client in prison now who was charged as a juvenile at the age of sixteen. His case was harmed by the actions of his older sister, who was eighteen at the time. He had started out with a juvenile record for skipping school and then graduated to misdemeanor marijuana possession. Next, the police alleged that he was part of a group of boys who tried to rob a convenience store in the same neighborhood where he lived and went to school. The convenience store had a video camera, which caught an image of the young man wearing a very distinctive coat. Carrying a photograph from the video of a boy in this coat, the police went to my client's house and knocked on the door.

When his older sister answered the door, the police held up a picture of their suspect and asked her, "Is this your brother?"

She said, "Yes. That's him. That's the coat he wore to school today."

So he got arrested and hauled away.

Her response should have been, "Why are you asking me that question?"

If they responded by saying, "We don't have to tell you that," she could have said, "Well, I don't have to answer your question. Come back with a subpoena or a warrant."

I understand that if the police are knocking at your door, inquiring about your child, you will most likely be freaked out, believing that something horrible has happened to him. But it's one thing to ask the police what happened to the boy, getting information you might need to ease your mind, and another matter entirely to start volunteering information about his actions and his whereabouts without legal counsel. You just never know how your statements might wind up being a vital factor in possibly sending an innocent person to jail.

That boy is now serving a ten-year sentence for armed robbery. Now certainly it is not his family's fault that this boy is in prison, but no one has an obligation to load the gun or supply the ammunition to get him there. It is absolutely essential that we educate the *entire* family about how to respond in these situations.

While that client was out on pre-trial release, I saw up close the challenges that families can introduce into the picture. Though his mother clearly cared what happened to this boy, she would have a few too many on the weekends and often get into minor confrontations with him. When he got her mad, she would berate and belittle him and threaten to call his pre-trial release supervisor or to call me in order to have him sent back to jail. One day she actually called the police because he did not want to take out the trash, or something equally ridiculous. After the boy was told she had called the police, he ran to the top of the apartment building where they lived and said he was going to jump off the roof because he was afraid of going back to jail.

When I asked her what she was doing, she said, "I just called them to scare him." Both the pre-trial release supervisor and I told her, "But you can't do that. When you called the police, it triggered a set of consequences for him. He's looking at being taken back into custody because he's out on bond. And he wasn't supposed to commit any new crimes. You said he assaulted you, so that's a new crime. Now he's back in jail."

Her response, while crying? "Oh, I didn't mean it."

Sometimes young men get pulled into some bad situations by their siblings—often, older brothers. I had a client who was a foster child in a household where there were two older boys who were also foster children. Of the three of them, my client was the one who had the bright future—he was a high school athlete who was doing well in school. The older brothers had already been involved in some thefts. One afternoon the three of them were together, riding around in a car with some other guys. The younger brother, who didn't know where the car came from, got dropped off back home while the other guys stayed in the car. As it turned out, the older brothers had stolen the car earlier in the day in a carjacking, using a gun and thus committing an armed robbery. When the other boys got arrested, someone in the car named my client as one of the passengers. For whatever reason, the police didn't hear the rest of his statement: "We dropped him off."

My client didn't know anything about the carjacking, but he wound up wallowing in the juvenile justice system. By the time I got the case, he had already been in the system for a year. Because of some miscommunication, it took me a while before I got a chance to go see him. I apologized profusely for taking so long to see him. I felt really bad about it.

"You don't have to apologize to me, Ms. Shipp," he said. "I have learned so much being in here about why I never want to be in here again. Thank you for coming late to see me, because otherwise I never would have known about this and could have gotten myself into trouble that would have resulted in me being here for a long time."

It blew me away; I actually started tearing up. I was able to get him a deal where he got credit for time served and he walked out. In his case, I believed him when he said he would never get into this kind of trouble again. He had plans to go into the military or go to college—either of which he'll be able to do because we were able to keep him in the juvenile system. Those records stay sealed unless he gets a felony charge as an adult—and even then they're opened only if he gets charged with something similar to armed robbery.

Sometimes I can see very clearly how a lack of proper parenting can have negative results. Recall Ricky, my fourteen-year-old client who was part of a group accused of gay bashing in Atlanta's Piedmont Park. Ricky was charged with robbery, assault, and battery. When the group, acting wild and super-aggressive, pushed a man to the ground and took his tennis shoes off his feet, they also used the word "faggots." That escalated this assault to the status of a hate crime and brought extensive media exposure, particularly since one of the men they assaulted was a gay activist who was in the park with his boyfriend. The case was in the headlines for months, with the faces of these boys all over the television screen.

Ricky's home life was not ideal. His mother would periodically show up in court and I always got the impression she was battling some sort of addiction, likely alcoholism. Sometimes Ricky's sister would come too, but he was very embarrassed by her. She was about sixteen and had a young baby and sometimes engaged in weird or inappropriate behavior. Ricky was a very angry young man. In fact, I actually had him evaluated for possible psychological issues because he demonstrated so much anger. After speaking with his mom—who was in her late 30s, early 40s—I learned that she preferred to view Ricky as a confidant, or a friend, rather than as a child she needed to provide for and protect.

I was able to get Ricky a deal in which his charges were transferred to juvenile court in exchange for him doing three years in juvenile court custody. I hoped that this plea would give Ricky an opportunity to attain his high school diploma and get his life on the right track. But I still worry about how Ricky fared once he got his life back and returned to an unstable home with no real parental supervision.

When it is time to assign blame for the state of the black community, for the plight of black boys, or for the educational failures of black children, the pointing fingers inevitably swing around to black mothers. In fact, when black boys become ensnared in the system, black mothers often point the finger at themselves.

If only I had....

As a defense attorney, I hear this all the time, this willingness of black mothers to take on responsibility for the burdens of their sons—indeed, of the entire black community. From my perch observing the devastation the criminal justice system can wreak on black families, I sometimes feel it is my job to assure mothers that they alone can't shoulder the responsibility for their children's plight. As we have discussed throughout this book, there are usually many factors at play that conspire to put a young black man behind bars.

As I've said before, many of my clients tend to be lower- to middle-class black kids who have gotten themselves into serious trouble for the first time. I've seen some troubling trends with these kids. Too many of them are desperate to be seen as authentic tough guys—what they consider in their media-warped minds to be "really black"—so they hitch themselves to the roughest kids they can find. By this backward way of thinking, any kind of middle-class status is a liability. I have a friend in New York whose net worth is considerable, but her son was so desperate to be a thug that he wound up getting killed.

Middle class, lower class, upper class: In every socioeconomic bracket, there are youngsters who get into trouble because they are acting like knuckleheads. Of course, that's no reason not to help them escape the jaws of the system, but sometimes you do want to shake some sense into them. I had a client who got into trouble with some other guys and while his co-defendants went to prison for four years, I was able to get him probation—with the assistance of his father, a proud, upstanding man who worked in a law enforcement capacity.

I told him, "Dad, you have to go before the court and you have to beg."

Judges see mothers begging all the time, but a begging father has a much different effect. So this man went before the judge and completely humbled himself. He blamed himself for his son's conduct and took responsibility for making sure his son corrected his misbehavior. It worked like a charm.

But unfortunately, the story didn't end there. About two years after that plea, the son was down in Texas and got into a confrontation with a cop. The young man yanked his arm away from the cop and got charged with a criminal trespass misdemeanor. A black male who is on probation cannot get away with yanking his arm away from the grip of a cop. Truthfully, any young black male who yanks his arm away from a cop, even one who isn't on probation, is likely to find himself in serious trouble. Instead of alerting his folks back in Georgia what had happened, he tried to handle it on his own. He hired an attorney in Texas and apparently didn't tell him about his history in Georgia. So this attorney decided against mounting a challenge and instead allowed the young man to take a plea for the trespass charge and time served in exchange for having the charge dismissed for hindering law enforcement, i.e., snatching his arm away from the cop.

The only problem with the plea deal? It violated his probation back in Georgia. So when he was returned to Georgia, the judge refused all pleas, revoked his first-offender status, and resentenced him to fifteen (rather than ten) years on probation. The Texas plea deal never should have occurred.

Before I close this chapter, I need to address a recent phenomenon that has quickly become something else for defense attorneys to worry about: social media. Social-media sites like Facebook and Twitter now play a huge role in prosecutions. Detectives are constantly going onto these sites to look at the accounts of young people charged with crimes to see what their social media affiliations are and to monitor the conversations of the suspects and their friends and family members. They're looking for gang affiliations, for symbols and mottoes that might link a young person to other criminal types—even something as simple or seemingly harmless as clicking "like" on a page or a post the detectives consider suspicious. They go trolling through the accounts of a suspect's siblings and friends, to see if anybody has made any comments about where the suspect was on the night of the alleged crime.

Young people—and even not-so-young people—must understand that everything you do on the Internet can ultimately be traced, and possibly used against you. It's not just the National Security Agency (NSA) that might be spying on you. You might have been joking about something, but in the harsh glare of a courtroom, your "joke" might suddenly take on a deeper significance. If you get charged with armed robbery and you clicked "like" on a graphic of a gun that had the words "Mo' money" printed underneath, don't be surprised if you're forced to explain yourself in a courtroom. You might think the connection between your alleged crime and the Facebook "like" is ridiculous, but all the prosecution has to do is make the jury believe there is some significance to it. As a defense attorney, I love putting my clients on the stand if they can get up there without hampering their defense. But the world of social media has given law enforcement a whole new frontier to use in attacking defendants.

So the advice here is clear: At all times, you (and your friends and family members) must be circumspect and careful. Live your life as if there are eyes on you at all times—especially online, where it's so easy for anything you ever post, comment on, or "like" to come to the attention of law enforcement.

Chapter 9: The Prison-Industrial Complex

The Vicious Cycle

To a remarkable degree, imprisoning black males in the United States has become big business, creating and sustaining hundreds of thousands of jobs across the nation and billions in profits for major corporations. In fact, the local, state, and federal governments in the US spent more than $74 billion on corrections in 2008, according to a report by the Center for Economic and Policy Research.

After years spent immersed in the system as a criminal defense attorney representing hundreds of young black males, I now recognize the devastating efficiency of the prison-industrial complex, an industry whose leading corporations are listed on the New York Stock Exchange and whose shareholders have a direct financial interest in seeing as many Americans locked up as possible.

While this chapter isn't as prescriptive as the others in the book, I believe the information here is essential, because it provides a context for a system that has become as destructive to the black community as a fast-moving, fatal virus.

Consider the case of the Corrections Corp. of America (CCA). A 2012 report in the online magazine *Business Insider* unveiled a presentation that CCA, one of the largest private corrections corporations in the nation, prepared for potential investors trumpeting the profit potential of the prison business. Noting that tight state budgets are making state governments increasingly interested in farming out their corrections facilities to the private sector—which currently runs about 10 percent of the nation's prisons—the prospectus pointed out that not only is the prison business "recession resistant," but it also holds "potential for accelerated growth in inmate populations following the recession." In addition, CCA noted that "demographic projections point to growing prison populations."

The CCA presentation went on to report that the high recidivism rates for American prisoners, in addition to US population growth, means that prisons will be an exciting profit opportunity for years to come. There will also be a growing demand for jail cells coming from immigration and customs enforcement, CCA pointed out.

A March 2012 story in *USA Today* described a proposal that CCA floated to prison officials in 48 states, offering to buy and manage public prisons at a substantial cost savings to the states. In order to do business with CCA, according to the proposal, the prisons would have to contain at least 1,000 beds and states would have to agree to maintain a 90 percent occupancy rate in the privately run prisons for at least 20 years.

Former secretary of corrections in Kansas Roger Werholtz noted that while states may be tempted by the quick infusion of cash, they "would be obligated to maintain these (occupancy) rates and subtle pressure would be applied to make sentencing laws more severe with a clear intent to drive up the population."

Adam Gopnik eloquently lashed the absurdity of this formula in a January 2012 piece in the *New Yorker*: "It's hard to imagine any greater disconnect between public good and private profit: The interest of private prisons lies not in the obvious social good of having the minimum necessary number of inmates but in having as many as possible, housed as cheaply as possible."

Michelle Alexander, whose book *The New Jim Crow: Mass Incarceration in the Age of Colorblindedness* has brought a new level of attention to this issue, acknowledged that when she was a young attorney, she looked askance at conspiracy theories about large-scale incarceration of African Americans. But over time, she began to realize that there was validity to the idea that many people and entities have benefitted from the explosion of the prison-industrial complex. In her book, she reveals the stunning fact that, contrary to popular belief, President Reagan announced the "War on Drugs" in 1982, several years *before* the crack epidemic came along and tore a hole in many black communities.

"The Reagan administration hired staff to publicize the emergence of crack cocaine in 1985 as part of a strategic effort to build public and legislative support for the war," Alexander writes. "The media campaign was an extraordinary success. Almost overnight, the media was saturated with images of black 'crack whores,' 'crack dealers,' and 'crack babies'—images that seemed to confirm the worst negative racial stereotypes about impoverished inner city residents."

Shockingly, as Alexander notes, illegal drug use was actually on the decline when Reagan announced the War on Drugs. After the implementation of the War on Drugs, with its mandatory sentencing guidelines and dramatically expanded focus on incarceration, the US penal population exploded from around 300,000 to more than 2 million, with drug convictions accounting for the majority of the increase. The US is the world's most prolific jailer, with rates of incarceration that dwarf every other developed country in the world. In the US, there were 716 prisoners per 100,000 people in the year 2013, according to a list compiled by the International Centre for Prison Studies, based at the UK's University of Essex. The next closest nation in the industrialized world was Russia at 475 prisoners per 100,000 people. Other developed nations with relatively high numbers were Thailand (398), Lithuania (329), South Africa (294), Iran (284) and Uruguay (281).

Another way to consider the numbers: Of the 10.2 million people in penal institutions across the globe, nearly a fourth of them were in the United States—but less than 5 percent of the world's 7.2 billion people live in the US.

"The scale and the brutality of our prisons are the moral scandal of American life," Adam Gopnik wrote in *The New Yorker.* "Every day, at least fifty thousand men—a full house at Yankee Stadium—wake in solitary confinement, often in 'supermax' prisons or prison wings, in which men are locked in small cells, where they see no one, cannot freely read and write, and are allowed out just once a day for an hour's solo 'exercise.' (Lock yourself in your bathroom and then imagine you have to stay there for the next ten years, and you will have some sense of the experience.)"

New York City, Arizona, Atlanta, Alabama, Washington state, Texas, Michigan, Pennsylvania, Los Angeles—across the nation, stories abound of police departments imposing arrest and ticket quotas on their officers to keep a steady stream of bodies flowing into jails—and income flowing into city and state coffers. In addition to being illegal in many states, these quotas blatantly encourage officers to find criminal behavior where none exists, and to take the easiest shortcuts to find suspects. In most places, those shortcuts mean preying on black and Hispanic youth, the population that mainstream society is most likely to believe is engaging in criminal behavior and that is least likely to rise up in protest.

Don't you think if the police decided to meet their quotas by arresting middle-aged white women, or even young white boys, most municipalities would make a loud hue and cry in protest?

In places like New York, lawsuits have been filed against the police department for using false arrests to meet ticket quotas. After listening to the testimony in a civil suit filed against the NYPD by a 46-year-old black woman, Carolyn Bryant, who claimed she was injured during her 2006 arrest, a Brooklyn jury found that city cops were motivated by arrest quotas. After the verdict, Bryant's lawyer, Seth Harris, said, "Other lawyers can now argue convincingly that the issue of quotas has been decided."

A major factor in the decision was the testimony of a NYPD police captain who testified that arrest numbers are a factor in assessing cops. Bryant claimed she was hurt when she confronted the cops who arrested her son on drug charges. Ultimately, the charges against her were dropped and the drug case against her son was dismissed.

In Atlanta, a local television station actually gained possession of an email sent from the head of the police union to members of the Atlanta Police Department, informing them the city budget now linked their future pay raises to the amount of revenue they were able to raise by writing tickets.

"Future pay increases are in our hands," union chief Ken Allen said in the 2013 email to Atlanta cops, which was obtained by the city's Channel 2 Action News.

I talked in Chapter 4 about how plea bargains often work to the detriment of defendants, but their benefit is clear to the prison-industrial complex. They virtually guarantee the steady stream of bodies that governments and private corporations like CCA desperately need. To house this steady stream, dying towns across the country have fought desperately for the opportunity to build and operate the prisons over the past 30 years, thinking they will bring jobs, visitors, and growth.

The federal Department of Agriculture tracked the prison boom and estimated that rural towns across America built an average of four prisons a year in the 1960s and 1970s, but by the 1990s had increased the pace to building up to 24 a year.

However, the prison boom proved to be an unreliable savior. These depressed towns came to rely on the prisons as a source of jobs, economic sustenance, and services, but neglected the need to attract other viable businesses.

"What we've seen in New York and other states is that one prison led to another prison and led to another prison, creating the notion that there's no other economic development option than to build prisons to foster stability in rural areas," Tracy Huling, an expert on prisons, told the *New York Times* in 2008.

Exacerbating the problem for these towns has been the dramatic decline in the nation's crime rate since the early 1990s, which in turn has reduced the need for more prison cells. Over the last few years, towns have resorted to fighting any efforts to shut their prisons down. In 2011, Littlefield, a small town in the northwest part of Texas, near Lubbock, had to auction off its Bill Clayton Detention Center for about half the $11 million it cost to build the jail in 1999. The town had to get rid of the jail, which had been vacant for two years, or risk defaulting on its loan. To pay for the jail, Littlefield had taken extraordinary steps like raising property taxes, increasing utility fees, and laying off city employees—all while watching its bond rating collapse.

From California to Virginia, towns across the country have gone through the same painful ordeal: they paid millions to build jails, hoping for a flood of bodies that never showed up to keep them in the black (pun definitely intended).

The tiny town of Hardin, Montana, even lobbied to accept sex offenders or possible terrorists from Guantanamo Bay at its state-of-the-art Two Rivers Detention Facility, which never housed a single prisoner after it was built in 2007. The bid failed and in

2008 the town defaulted on $27 million in bonds, according to the Associated Press.

The state of Louisiana took a unique approach to the prison-as-profit formula. In the 1990s, when the state was ordered by a federal court to reduce prison overcrowding, sheriffs lobbied for prison construction in parishes around the state, promising future profits. With plenty of capacity that must be filled, wardens in Louisiana now make daily calls around the state to sheriffs' jails in search of fresh inmates. Urban areas with an abundance of offenders, such as New Orleans and Baton Rouge, wind up shipping many prisoners out to remote parishes, which are desperate to keep the prisoners and the profits coming. Sheriffs use the profits to buy new squad cars, guns, and laptops, according to a 2012 story by Cindy Chang in the New Orleans *Times-Picayune*.

That story quotes Fred Schoonover, deputy warden of the 522-bed Tensas Parish Detention Center in northeast Louisiana, who has to wheel and deal everyday to keep his jail filled. "We struggle. I stay on the phone a lot, calling all over the state, trying to hustle a few," Schoonover says.

With the flow of prisoners receding, increasingly desperate officials have been reaching into a new potential source for their inmates: schools. The term "school-to-prison pipeline" has been used increasingly to describe systems where youngsters are criminalized and locked up for committing acts that in a previous era would barely get a rise out of the principal. Some of the examples of this pipeline in action are especially egregious. In Wilkes-Barre, Pennsylvania, two judges pleaded guilty in 2009 to accepting $2.6 million in bribes in exchange for sending juvenile defendants to local, privately run facilities, regardless of whether they were guilty or innocent or how severe their supposed crimes were. The scheme was overseen by the Mid-Atlantic Youth Service Corporation, which specializes in private prisons for juvenile offenders. More than 5,000 kids were sent through their courtrooms and to prison for crimes as minor as stealing DVDs from Walmart and trespassing in vacant buildings, according to CNN. After their guilty pleas, one of the judges was sentenced to 17½ years in prison; the other got 28 years. But thousands of kids' lives were destroyed by the greed of the adults around them.

Meridian, Mississippi, became infamous in June 1964 as the home base of civil-rights workers James Chaney, Michael Schwerner, and Andrew Goodman, who were killed for trying to register blacks to vote. Meridian was also recently home to an episode of egregious disregard for the lives of children. Meridian set up a school-to-prison pipeline that sent a steady stream of kids into the city's juvenile justice system for infractions as minor as wearing the wrong color socks, talking back to a teacher, and coming to school without wearing a belt—kids as young as ten, and all of them black, according to a story in Colorlines.com.

Things got so bad in Meridian that the federal Department of Justice filed a lawsuit against the city in 2012, alleging that the pipeline violates the due process rights of young people by sending them into the criminal justice system without even telling them what charges had been made against them.

"[D]efendants engage in a pattern or practice of unlawful conduct through which they routinely and systematically arrest and incarcerate children, including for minor school rule infractions, without even the most basic procedural safeguards, and in violation of these children's constitutional rights," the DOJ's 37-page complaint reads. Meridian's years of systemic abuse punish youth "so arbitrarily and severely as to shock the conscience."

Once those children were in the juvenile justice system, they were denied their basic constitutional rights. They were handcuffed by the police and incarcerated for days without a hearing and subsequently warehoused in jail without understanding what they had been accused of doing.

In this country, we love to pay lip service to how much we care about kids and how strongly we believe they represent the future. But in this instance, the town of Meridian seemed filled with contempt for its young people. In Meridian, young people were walking dollar signs—especially the ones with brown faces.

Gloria Green's son was locked up so often in his eighth-grade year that he was held back a year. "It was mind-boggling. My son loved school, and to be kicked out as much as he was, one year he just couldn't catch up."

In its suit, the Department of Justice charged Meridian's police department with operating a de facto "taxi service," shuttling students out of school and into youth jails.

Another one of the shocking ways law enforcement can abuse its power and keep the revenue flowing is through asset forfeiture. When Congress passed the Comprehensive Crime Control Act in 1984 as part of the War on Drugs, it allowed law-enforcement agencies to pocket the proceeds from forfeitures for which they were responsible. This meant local police who provided assistance on big federal drug cases were rewarded with a large percentage of the proceeds, through a program called Equitable Sharing. The process soon exploded, driven by a new profit motive. Proceeds raked in by the federal DOJ went from $27 million in 1985 to $4.2 billion in 2012, according to a 2013 expose in *The New Yorker* magazine. Agencies could take in more money and reduce public spending at the same time—surely dispatches from a Republican fantasy.

In 1989, US Attorney General Richard Thornburgh famously said, "It's now possible for a drug dealer to serve time in a forfeiture-financed prison after being arrested by agents driving a forfeiture-provided automobile while working in a forfeiture-funded sting operation."

According to a 2013 story in *The New Yorker* by Sarah Stillman, police officers in Tulsa, Oklahoma, have been spotted driving around in a Cadillac Escalade stenciled with the words, "This used to be a drug dealer's car, now it's ours!"

What started as a means of going after drug kingpins eventually changed into something much uglier: The system was used to seize cash and property from regular citizens. Law enforcement officers just started taking people's stuff—people who hadn't been convicted, or in many cases even accused, of committing crimes. Not surprisingly, most of the victims tended to be poor and black or Hispanic.

"We all know the way things are right now—budgets are tight," Steve Westbrook, the executive director of the Sheriffs' Association of Texas, said in *The New Yorker* piece. "It's definitely a valuable asset to law enforcement, for purchasing equipment and getting things you normally wouldn't be able to get to fight crime."

In cities such as Philadelphia, according to Stillman, law enforcement routinely seizes homes related to unproven minor drug crimes—such as when the homeowner's child or grandchild is accused of selling some weed.

"For real-estate forfeitures, it's overwhelmingly African-Americans and Hispanics," Louis Rulli, who runs a clinic at the University of Pennsylvania Law School, told *The New Yorker*. "It has a very disparate race and class impact."

Rulli ruefully noted that when then-Philadelphia Eagles football coach Andy Reid's sons were caught running a large-scale drug operation from their father's mansion in the Philly area, no law enforcement official dared lift a finger to seize Reid's house.

Many state legislatures, facing painful fiscal crises, moved to make the forfeiture statutes even more nimble, more voracious, and to make it easier for law enforcement to use the revenue any way they wanted. In some Texas counties, nearly 40 percent of police budgets come from forfeiture, according to *The New Yorker*. And usually the victims are too poor and powerless to fight back.

"There's this myth that they're cracking down on drug cartels and kingpins," Lee McGrath of the Institute for Justice, an expert on Georgia's extensive use of the forfeiture laws, told *The New Yorker*. "In reality, it's small amounts, where people aren't entitled to a public defender, and can't afford a lawyer, and the only rational response is to walk away from your property, because of the infeasibility of getting your money back."

McGrath said 58 local, county, and statewide police forces in Georgia brought in $2.76 million in forfeitures in 2011, and that more than half the items taken were worth less than $650.

By building a profit motive into the law-enforcement apparatus, states and localities have created a monster capable of devouring anyone in its path too powerless to get out of the way.

States have also taken to using the probation system as a fundraising mechanism. Money-starved towns across the country have hired for-profit businesses to collect cash from the citizenry for fines and fees accrued from the writing of tickets. When poor folks can't pay the hundreds and sometimes thousands of dollars in fees that can accumulate from something as simple as an unpaid parking or speeding ticket, they might find themselves sitting in a jail cell.

"With so many towns economically strapped, there is growing pressure on the courts to bring in money rather than mete out justice," Lisa W. Borden, a partner at Baker, Donelson, Bearman, Caldwell & Berkowitz, a large law firm in Birmingham, Alabama, told the *New York Times* in 2012. "The companies they hire are aggressive. Those arrested are not told about the right to counsel or asked whether they are indigent or offered an alternative to fines and jail. There are real constitutional issues at stake."

With misdemeanors, lawyers are rarely involved, meaning people have no protection when they wade unwittingly into a system that can send them to jail if they don't follow the rules. The *Times* called it a "legal Twilight Zone," as the private companies find creative ways to milk citizens for the revenue they promise the towns.

The *Times* tells the story of Richard Garrett, a former US Steel employee who had spent a total of 24 months in jail and owed $10,000 for traffic and license violations that began a decade ago.

"The Supreme Court has made clear that it is unconstitutional to jail people just because they can't pay a fine," Birmingham attorney William M. Dawson, who filed a lawsuit on behalf of Garrett, told the *Times*.

In the state of Georgia, about three dozen for-profit probation companies operate in hundreds of courts, locking up Georgians for failing to pay their fines.

"These companies are bill collectors, but they are given the authority to say to someone that if he doesn't pay, he is going to jail," said John B. Long, a lawyer in Augusta, Georgia, who has challenged the system. "There are things like garbage collection where private companies are OK. No one's liberty is affected. The closer you get to locking someone up, the closer you get to a constitutional issue."

"Many states are imposing new and often onerous 'user fees' on individuals with criminal convictions," according to a 2010 study from the Brennan Center for Justice at the New York University School of Law. "Yet far from being easy money, these fees impose severe—and often hidden—costs on communities, taxpayers, and indigent people convicted of crimes. They create new paths to prison for those unable to pay their debts and make it harder to find employment and housing as well as to meet child-support obligations."

Stephen B. Bright, president of the Southern Center for Human Rights and a professor at Yale Law School, said that with the private companies seeking a profit, with courts in need of income, and with the most vulnerable caught up in the system, "we end up balancing the budget on the backs of the poorest people in society."

When discussing the nation's 2.3 million prisoners, at some point we must examine our ridiculously high recidivism rate. Most studies show that around 40 percent of people released from prison wind up returning within three years. This number says more about the harsh world and scarce opportunities these former offenders face on the outside than their predilection for crime. In addition to the difficulty of finding meaningful employment, they have to contend with a long list of parole restrictions and requirements that make it inevitable that many of them will wind up back in a cell.

In most states, nearly a third of those who return to prison are sent back because of "technical" violations, which means they have violated parole rules, rather than committing another crime. What are these technical violations? Many states require parolees to pay a monthly "supervision fee" or a "victim fee" of amounts typically around $30 a month. Failure to pay the fee, which may prove difficult for ex-offenders who are having a hard time finding meaningful employment, could result in a parole violation and possibly even a return to prison.

Many parolees are forced to submit to electronic monitoring, which means having a receiver attached to your ankle that sends a GPS signal back to your parole supervisor notifying him of your whereabouts at all times. The parolees also must pay a fee for the device. While parolees subject to electronic monitoring technically are able to maintain employment, access community-based treatment, perform community service work, address medical issues, and attend religious functions, the logistics of such a life are tedious and debilitating.

Brian Banks, the ex-football player who was wrongly convicted of rape and spent 5 years in a California prison and 5 years out on parole, described the psychological damage he suffered from wearing the ankle bracelet 24 hours a day for 5 years. Not only did he go an entire five years in the California heat without ever wearing shorts outside or going to the beach, but he was also reluctant to enter into any kind of an intimate relationship because of his ankle hardware. And forget about going to a nightclub or anywhere with a metal detector.

Then there was the pressure of rushing back home in the evening to recharge the bracelet, which had to be plugged into an outlet every 12 hours for recharging—a process which itself took an hour. On the few occasions when he accidentally fell asleep at night and forgot to plug it into the charger, he would be awakened in the middle of the night by the violent shaking of the battery-depleted bracelet. During the inevitable phone call from his parole officer, he'd have to plead with the officer to let it slide and not haul him in for a parole violation, which could result in his being sent back to prison.

"It's a trap, designed for you to reoffend," Banks said in an interview.

In their 2009 book, *Prison Profiteers: Who Makes Money from Mass Incarceration*, prison-rights activists Tara Herivel and Paul Wright compiled essays that chronicled the mind-bending web of entities that profit from the prison-industrial complex—providers of everything from prison transportation services to medical services, from food to telephone calls. The investment banks, the guard unions, the makers of stun guns, the US military (which heavily relies on the labor of prisoners)—all are part of the prison-industrial complex's massive interlocking network that spans across industries and touches millions across the nation. Considering the profits derived from this billion-dollar business, it's easy to see why so many Americans are invested in this country continuing to lock up as many people as possible.

The 2013 video series *Prison Profiteers* examined the businesses and industries that profit from mass incarceration and the impact they have on everyday Americans. For instance, the telephone provider Global Tel Link (GTL) makes more than

$500 million a year by exploiting the need for inmates and their families to talk on the telephone. The company charges exorbitant rates of up to $1.13 per minute for simple collect phone calls from prison. Like other telecommunications companies involved in the incarceration system, GTL wins its contracts by offering a kickback—or "commission"—to the prison or jail systems it serves, with the amount of the kickback based on a percentage of the revenue generated by the phone calls. According to a 2011 study in *Prison Legal News*, "[The] commissions dwarf all other considerations and are a controlling factor when awarding prison phone contracts." So that means the higher a kickback, according to *The Nation*, the more likely a company is to win the contract.

The video series profiled a 9-year-old boy from Nashville, Kenny Davis, one of the 2.7 million US children who have incarcerated parents, who rarely speaks to his father because his mother can't afford frequent calls from the private prison where his father is housed.

"All the evidence shows that prisoners who maintain close family ties fare better upon release," the series pointed out. "Making it harder for prisoners to stay connected with their families is not only needlessly punitive and cruel, it is unwise from a public safety standpoint."

The healthcare of inmates has long been an area where neglect and abuse run rampant, in a nation that doesn't mind having its prisoners treated as if they are less than human. California, whose prisons are notoriously overcrowded, was forced to pay $585,000 to a man who lost an eye while locked up on a parole violation in 2008. The man had glaucoma and begged for his medication. Prison officials ignored him—until his cornea burst.

New York state had its prison abuses chronicled by the *New York Times* in 2005 after two prisoners died in upstate hospitals within two months of each other at jails under the medical supervision of Prison Health Services, which had denied medical attention and medication to both deceased inmates.

Prison Profiteers shines a disturbing spotlight on Corizon, the nation's largest provider of prison healthcare. The video profiles Frankie Barton, a Tucson woman whose incarcerated son is sick with hepatitis C, which Corizon has discouraged treating in its prisons for years.

"My son's being told they have no protocol for treating anybody with hepatitis C," Barton says.

In Louisville, Kentucky, seven sick prisoners died at Metro Corrections, a Corizon jail. Afterward, six employees quit their jobs "amid an investigation by the jail that found that the workers 'may' have contributed" to two of the deaths, according to a report in *The Nation*.

When former ACLU attorney Will Harrell inspected a facility in Coke County, Texas, run by the mammoth private company GEO Group, he was disgusted by what he found.

"There was an infestation of insects everywhere you looked, including the kitchen," he said, according to *The Nation*. "Insects in the food. It was horrible."

Donald Weeks, who spent ten months locked up at GEO-run East Mississippi Correctional Facility, was quoted in *Prison Profiteers* describing the unconscionable sewage problems.

"The stench was so bad in there, I couldn't eat anymore," he said.

Too often when we talk about problems that plague African Americans and other people of color in this country, we fail to enlarge our view to the big picture. We focus too much on individual responsibility and personal failures without taking to task the systems and the institutions that control our lives from on high, like puppeteers manipulating marionettes. In this chapter, I have tried to demonstrate that when it comes to the mind-boggling number of African Americans who are ensnared in the nation's prison-industrial complex, a staggering number of individuals and businesses are profiting from our mass incarceration. While each of us as individuals may not be in a position to fight the system, each of us *can* pressure our elected officials to dismantle these institutions and take the profit motive out of incarceration. That would be a huge step toward rescuing our communities and our young black males from the greedy jaws of this incredibly destructive system.

Chapter 10: Your Guide to Navigating the System

WHAT FOLLOWS IS A BASIC SUMMARY of the advice, lessons, and messages contained in the previous nine chapters. Use this for quick reference to access key information about how to deal with the criminal justice system.

CHAPTER 1: OFFICER FRIENDLY ISN'T YOUR FRIEND

Everything You Need to Know about Racial Profiling

Though the US Constitution and US courts prohibit racial profiling, the practice is still common across the nation.

❑ **Though blacks and whites use marijuana in roughly the** same proportions, a report by the ACLU found that in 2010 blacks were 3.73 times more likely than whites to be arrested for marijuana possession—a "crime" that isn't even a crime anymore in parts of the country that have legalized marijuana. In Washington, DC, blacks were an astounding eight times more likely than whites to be arrested for marijuana possession.

❑ **Drug possession cases, which often begin with some type** of racial profiling practiced by the police, are now the lifeblood—or the cancer, depending on where you sit—of the American criminal justice system. According to the FBI's annual Crime in the US report, among the 12.2 million arrests in the US in 2012, only property crime (1.64 million) was more common than drug possession (1.55 million). In recent years, drug possession has often meant marijuana possession, as nearly half of the drug possession arrests in the FBI report were for marijuana.

❑ **The most common form of racial profiling occurs when a** police officer pulls over one or a group of young black males in an automobile. The vehicle stop is the bugle call that initiates the entire legal drama that many of us have come to describe as "driving while black."

In the minds of the police, everything is about justifying the stop. As long as they have a justification, they can legally stop anyone they want. One of the officer's primary motivations during every stop is to find the justification to make the stop rise to the legal definition of "reasonable."

❑ **A growing body of research has highlighted the likelihood** of inaccuracies in eyewitness identifications. (The Innocence Project estimates that eyewitness misidentification plays a role in nearly 75 percent of convictions overturned through DNA testing, making it the single greatest cause of wrongful convictions in the nation.) When researchers conduct controlled experiments to test the accuracy of eyewitness identifications, they have found that eyewitnesses incorrectly identify strangers at about the same rate as they identify them correctly. Compounding the problem is the fact that people are much more likely to misidentify a stranger of another race.

❑ **Most problematically for black males, white people appear** to have an especially hard time correctly identifying African Americans, according to researchers. Despite all of these disturbing problems, eyewitness identification remains the fuel that powers most law-enforcement investigations and prosecutions.

❑ **While it's unfair to be singled out by the police and possibly** placed under arrest due to general suspicion of black people—not to mention arbitrary, painful, and enraging—it is crucial to hold it together in this scenario. You must exercise discipline and self-control. If the police are loading you into the squad car because they think you've committed a crime, then your anger and frustration in their eyes might be translated as guilt and desperation. In addition, you don't want to give them a reason to file any more charges against you—or worse, to hurt you.

❑ **The US Constitution includes several amendments that** are of vital importance when you are in police custody. It's your attorney's job to determine whether any of your constitutional rights have been violated. The Fourth Amendment grants you the right to be free of unreasonable searches and seizures. The Fifth Amendment protects your right to your life and liberty through the exercise of due process. Remaining silent and only speaking when you absolutely have to while in police custody is always a good policy. Too often, individuals give up their constitutional protections by opening their mouths and letting the words flow without an attorney being present. The Constitution does you no good unless you use it.

❏ **There are numerous ways African Americans become tar-**
gets simply because of race. Many African-American men and
women have experienced "shopping while black," when retailers
see an African American shopping in their store as a likely thief
rather than a paying customer. Research has shown that white
women in their forties engage in more shoplifting than other demographic groups. However, they don't get caught in the same
proportions, most likely because they aren't being watched in the
same ways.

❏ **Even when controlling for socioeconomic status, African-**
American students are suspended and expelled at two to three
times the rate of white students, according to researchers. And
the consequences of these suspensions are severe, because it often becomes the first step in what has been called the school-to-
prison pipeline: 49 percent of students who entered high-school
with three suspensions on their record eventually dropped out of
school, according to a study by Johns Hopkins University. This
leads to another astounding statistic: black male high-school
dropouts are 38 times more likely to be incarcerated than black
males with a four-year college degree.

❏ **Education is the best way to wriggle free from these traps.**
But this doesn't mean just academic performance. Young black
males must educate themselves as much as possible about search
and seizure laws, probable cause, and all the other the rules and
regulations that control the actions of law enforcement.

CHAPTER 2: SILENCE IS GOLDEN

How to Handle Stop-and-Frisk and Illegal Searches

❑ **The stop is the logical consequence of racial profiling.** The officer must have a "reasonable and articulable" suspicion that criminal activity is afoot. If he doesn't, according to the law, he shouldn't have made the stop.

❑ **In an 8–1 decision, the Supreme Court's landmark 1968** *Terry v. Ohio* case ruled that the Fourth Amendment prohibition on unreasonable searches and seizures is not violated when a police officer stops a suspect on the street and frisks him without probable cause, as long as the officer has a reasonable suspicion that the person has committed, is committing, or is about to commit a crime, and has a reasonable belief that the person "may be armed and presently dangerous."

The court ruled that for their own protection, police may perform a quick surface search of a person's outer clothing for weapons if they have reasonable suspicion that the person is armed. According to the court, this reasonable suspicion must be based on "specific and articulable facts," and not merely upon an officer's hunch. Importantly, in his concurring opinion, Justice Byron White pointed out that although the police may direct questions at a person they have stopped under the proper circumstances, "the person stopped is not obliged to answer, answers may not be compelled, and refusal to answer furnishes no basis for an arrest, although it may alert the officer to the need for continued observation."

❑ **The worst thing a black male can do when stopped is say** things that make him appear to be a potential suspect. In other words, when stopped by police, the one thing that most people should do is to shut up. Many people talk themselves into criminal charges, rather than out of them. Again: Silence is the best response when stopped by the police.

What to Do If Stopped While Driving

- Pull over safely to the side of the road if you see a police flashing lights behind you
- If the officer asks where you're coming from, politely ask why you were stopped—remember, the Supreme Court has ruled that the officer must have a reasonable suspicion based on "specific and articulable facts" that a person who's been stopped is armed or has committed, is committing, or is about to commit a crime
- Answer the officer's questions as succinctly as possible, without embellishment
- Always have your identification handy; if the officer asks for your license and registration, get his permission to reach for them— you don't want him thinking you may be reaching for a weapon
- If they ask for permission to search your car, politely refuse
- If the officer tells you to get out of the car, do as he says—and if he puts you up against the car, *stay there*
- If police insist on searching the vehicle, remain silent while they are doing so
- Most importantly, even though you will almost certainly be outraged, don't give the police any attitude or reason to claim you were hostile or belligerent, because that's the quickest way to escalate the encounter

What to Do If Stopped While Walking

- By all means, never run from the police
- Police have the right to stop you and ask your name, so if this happens, politely tell the police your name
- Beyond that initial question, the US Constitution guarantees each of us the right to remain silent, so don't volunteer any additional information

- Because the stop is usually a pretext for the officer to have close contact with you in order to see if you are under the influence of alcohol or illegal drugs or in possession of contraband, be as polite and courteous as possible
- Don't curse or antagonize the officer
- There is a good chance the officer is stopping you because he believes you match the description for a suspect who did something nearby—which may be as general as "young, black, male, short hair." If that's the case, you won't be able to talk your way out of it, so don't say anything

What to Do If Arrested

- Be polite and don't contradict the officer's reason for arresting you
- Try to stay calm and resist the urge to become belligerent
- Use every ounce of your willpower to resist the urge to say something to convince them to release you—it's not going to happen, and anything you say will likely just make things worse
- As soon as you can, call someone who can hire you an attorney to come to the station as soon as possible
- If your parents or family members come to assist you, resist the urge to explain to them everything that happened, as the police are likely recording every word you say to them

What to Do If You See Police Harassing a Friend

- Don't confront the police
- Try to get your friend to remain as calm and nonthreatening as possible. Keep telling him, "Calm down and be quiet"
- Create enough distance between you and the police officer so that the officer doesn't perceive himself to be in danger
- As surreptitiously as possible, turn on the recording device on your cell phone. Having a video or audio recording of the encounter may become extremely important
- Do not intervene, because there's nothing you can do except escalate the encounter and make it worse
- Make sure you get the badge number of the officer involved

❏ **As a result of New York City's controversial "stop-and-frisk"** policing, the NYPD conducted 4.4 million stops between January 2004 and June 2012, but just 6 percent resulted in arrests and 6 percent generated summonses, according to data compiled by the New York Civil Liberties Union. That means in 88 percent of those 4.4 million stops, the person stopped was doing nothing wrong. And while more than half of all people stopped were frisked, only 1.5 percent of the frisks uncovered weapons. Blacks or Hispanics were stopped in 83 percent of these cases, although they make up just over half of New York City's population.

In August 2013, US District Court Judge Shira Scheindlin delivered a scathing decision that lashed New York City officials who had "turned a blind eye" to evidence that officers carried out searches in a "racially discriminatory manner," thus violating individuals' right to privacy and equal treatment under the law. Scheindlin said the city was not in compliance with what is required under the Constitution, and she appointed a monitor to oversee the NYPD's compliance.

As a result of this ruling, if a city has a policy—whether written or just de facto—that has a disproportionate impact on a protected group like African Americans, that policy can be attacked in court, and the city might find itself subject to remedies such as those imposed in New York City. This means that if a police officer stops someone simply for being the same color and gender as the majority of the criminals that officer has arrested, then that officer has just violated the US Constitution.

CHAPTER 3: **THE HISTORY BETWEEN POLICE AND BLACK MALES**

From Slave Patrols to the KKK—to Today

❑ **A close reading of US history reveals a stark fact: Law en-**forcement in the US has always been an enemy of black people. To a large extent, law enforcement as it exists in the US, particularly in the American South, was *created* as a means to control, punish, and monitor black people.

❑ **By tracing the straight line from slave patrols to post-**Emancipation policing to the KKK to modern police forces, African Americans can better understand the nature of the relationship we currently suffer through with law enforcement in the US. This superior understanding allows us to prepare our black boys and girls for the animosity they are likely to face from police when they step out from under their parents' watchful eye. History can help save our lives.

❑ **Throughout the literature on slavery, one constant remains:** the white community's ever-present fear. While poisonings were a more personalized form of retribution—capable of striking terror in the hearts of slave owners as they watched their bondsmen and bondswomen prepare their meals, fetch their water, and raise their children—it was the slave insurrections that truly evoked fear throughout the white community.

❑ **Towns like Wilmington and Charleston created their own** night-watch groups to control slave behavior.

❑ **A major preoccupation of Southern white men during the** Civil War years was what might happen to their women, children, and plantations if they left the slaves untended. This fear led them to exempt from war duty any man who owned or supervised 20 slaves or more—an exemption that came to be known as the "20-nigger law."

❑ **Southern whites, feeling frustrated by their powerlessness** and emboldened by their vague fears of newly freed blacks, flocked to join the Ku Klux Klan, which was started in 1865. Whites quickly saw the vigilante group as a way to scare the freedmen into political and social submission. In some Southern counties, the sheriff, deputies, and all important local officials were members of the Klan.

❑ **Many former slaves reported that, in terms of law enforcement,** things were actually less brutal during slavery than they were after Emancipation.

❑ **Institutional habits and practices get passed on from generation** to generation. By deed and description, police veterans train their successors. The grandson of a police officer who joined the force at age 20 in Charleston or Atlanta or Boston in 1905 could wind up training officers in 1995 (with the assumption that the grandfather, his son, and his grandson each spent 30 years on the force).

❑ **In the early decades of the century, dozens of African** Americans were lynched every year—often with the involvement of law enforcement. Cities like Atlanta, Philadelphia, East St. Louis, and Springfield, Illinois, exploded in deadly race riots—often triggered by some horrific act committed by a white police officer.

❑ **A 2013 report from the Malcolm X Grassroots Movement** concluded that police officers, security guards, or self-appointed vigilantes killed at least 313 African Americans in 2012, which means a rate of one every 28 hours.

CHAPTER 4: **THE PLEA BARGAIN TRAP**

How to Fight It

❑ **In the US, 97 percent of federal cases and 94 percent of** state cases never make it to trial because of the plea bargain. The plea-bargain process sends a steady stream of bodies into the system, keeping jobs secure and money flowing.

❑ **Numerous studies have shown that black defendants fare** much worse than white defendants in the plea-bargain process, routinely receiving lengthier sentences than whites accused of the same crimes. In combination with the imposition of mandatory minimum sentences, the plea deal is one of the primary reasons why the black prison population has exploded while actual crime in the US has plummeted.

❑ **Prosecutors admit that they routinely "load up" charges** against defendants, throwing a stack of crimes with harsh sentences at them—crimes that the prosecutors know they wouldn't be able to prove in court—in order to force them to plead guilty to lesser offenses.

❑ **Plea bargains are the expected result for the drug cases that** flood most of the nation's courts. With drug cases, it's especially important to know the facts before you start mulling over a plea bargain. Drug cases are very fact sensitive, meaning the details are crucial. For instance, when a car full of black males gets pulled over and the police get permission to search the vehicle, or claim they have a reasonable, articulable suspicion that criminal activity is afoot, everybody in the car usually gets charged if they find drugs under the driver's seat. Depending on their criminal records, everybody's likely to get the same plea offer—five years on probation. But taking that probated sentence might be the wrong decision for the passengers in the above scenario, who have a good argument that they had no idea the drugs were even in the car.

❑ **Experts estimate that 2 to 5 percent, and probably more, of** the people currently in prison are innocent, largely because of the plea-bargain system. This means tens of thousands of innocent people, a huge majority of them black and brown men, are languishing in prison cells.

❑ **Facts are facts. Sometimes the facts are overwhelmingly** against defendants who strongly assert their innocence, which makes a guilty verdict at trial very likely. In such cases, defendants should strongly consider a plea bargain.

❑ **The generosity of the plea offer greatly depends on where** the alleged crime was committed.

❑ **The plea offer is one instance where a client has to be par-**ticularly careful when represented by a public defender. Because of the sheer number of cases they handle, public defenders cannot spend much time on each. This means a public defender may be more likely to grab a plea offer than a private attorney handling the same case. Make sure a public defender's recommendation to accept a plea is not just a quick way to get your case off his to-do list.

❑ **You need to do everything in your power to make sure you** have someone representing you who is pursuing your innocence as if her own freedom depended on it.

CHAPTER 5: GET ME JOHNNIE COCHRAN

When You Don't Have Cash to Hire a High-Profile Lawyer

❑ **The modern apparatus of the public defender evolved in** the wake of the 1963 Supreme Court decision in *Gideon vs. Wainwright*, which established that state courts are required under the Fourteenth Amendment to provide lawyers to represent defendants in criminal cases who can't afford their own attorneys. But because of the enormous number of indigent clients, too many receive inadequate counsel.

❑ **While many extremely able attorneys work as public de-**fenders, it is nearly impossible for many of them to give each case the attention it deserves, due to caseloads that could easily soar into the hundreds. It is not humanly possible for any attorney to investigate, draft motions, argue motions, do legal research, interview witnesses, and prepare for trial with that kind of caseload.

❑ **Every single day, Americans are incorrectly accused of** crimes they didn't commit, or charged excessively for an offense they may have committed, or suffer an egregious range of other mistakes that occur during the criminal-justice process. Walking into the police station with a "once you're arrested, I'm washing my hands of you" attitude would be an enormous disservice to one's child and to the preparation of that child's defense.

❑ **There are many ways that a client can tell whether his at-**torney is providing him a rigorous defense:

Are your phone calls being returned?
Are motions being filed?
Have you been asked personal questions about yourself?

❑ **In most cases, if you tell the court you and your family** want to hire another attorney to represent you, the judge will continue the case to a later date. A judge can't force you to take a plea.

❑ **Whether you are represented by a public defender or a** private attorney, there are still things you can do to help your case. The most important? *Tell your attorney everything!* Every tiny bit of information needs to be passed on to your attorney, even things that seem irrelevant. You must provide every shred of information about your background. Were you abused as a child? Did you experience some sort of deprivation? Were you in special education because of some learning disability or psychological or emotional problems? Many young people who go on to commit crimes have shown signs of some sort of developmental or psychological disorder that might prove relevant to the defense. If your lawyer is aware of some of these early issues, she might be able to get you diagnosed, which could greatly help your case.

❑ **When the court appoints a private attorney to represent** you, you don't have any control over which attorney you get. It's the luck of the draw.

❑ **Word-of-mouth will always be the best method of finding** an attorney. Start asking around, and it won't take long to find someone willing to share an experience they've had with an attorney. Parents usually hire the attorney if the defendant is under the age of 26. Try asking family members, friends, or colleagues.

❑ **There are also quite a few websites where you can find list-**ings of lawyers, such as martindale.com, avvo.com, and justia.com. Use your state's bar association resources to find out if particular attorneys have had any disciplinary actions taken against them.

❏ **When they have enough time to devote to cases, some** public defenders can be extremely effective, because they've seen everything under the sun. A private attorney may not have seen as many armed robberies as a public defender has. The more you see it, the more you understand it, and the better you can defend it.

CHAPTER 6: GET A HAIRCUT

The Black Male Goes to Trial

❏ **For black male defendants, a primary goal should be to** make sure you look as little as possible like the faces the jury sees in the nightly black male crime parade on the TV news. If the members of the jury look over to the defense table and see someone they believe looks like a criminal, you are doomed. If they see a scared but earnest and honest young man, you have a chance.

❏ **Dreadlocks, tattoos, long fingernails—all of these must be** shorn or covered as much as possible.

❏ **Though you can take educated guesses, you can't really** predict with absolute certainty what a jury will do, and how a particular juror will respond to you and your client. Just because a juror is white, you can't assume he or she will be your enemy. On the flip side, you can't make any assumptions about what a black juror will do either.

❏ **Juries pay close attention to the relationship between at-** torneys and their clients. If an attorney sits next to the client and never interacts with him, never touches him, and never makes eye contact, the jury is going to get the impression that the attorney doesn't like the client. That's going to be a problem for the client during jury deliberations.

CHAPTER 7: JESUS...SOMEBODY...PLEASE HELP!

Never Give Up Hope

❑ **Sometimes even the most daunting circumstances can shift** in an instant. The message here is simple: Never give up hope.

❑ **These days, more and more youthful conduct that in previ-**ous decades would have elicited barely a yawn from the authorities has now been criminalized. Police today aggressively patrol the streets looking not just for criminals, but also for young people engaged in bad behavior.

❑ **You should be extra careful at all times about who you as-**sociate with. If your gut tells you a situation feels wrong, trust your gut and get the hell out of there. Otherwise, you could easily find yourself in a predicament where you know you're innocent, but from the outside your innocence looks extremely questionable and even harder to prove.

CHAPTER 8: FAMILIES

Got to Be There

❑ **The one thing families must remember when they learn** that a loved one has been arrested can be summed up in a simple, seven-letter word: Support. A young person never needs the support of family more than when he is up against the prison-industrial complex. And the best way for the family to offer that support is to consult with a lawyer before making any statements to the police or anybody else about the case in question.

❑ **Family members—Mom, Dad, siblings, cousins—all need** to understand that you don't have to talk to the police just be-

cause the police ask. You don't have to go down to the police station and make statements—statements that have the potential to
incriminate your child in a crime—just because the police invite
you down.

❑ **When called to the police station to talk to your child, your**
best response is a form of the following: *I prefer to do what's best
for my child and get him an attorney. Let him know we'll be there to
see him soon accompanied by his attorney.*

❑ **In the United States, someone is arrested every two seconds.**
There's a drug arrest every 19 seconds. But being arrested doesn't
necessarily mean your child has committed a crime. And they
don't stop being our children just because they've been arrested
and charged with a crime. You never stop being a parent. Parental
love and support should include getting them adequate counsel if
they get in trouble.

❑ **When a child is being taken into custody, anything that's**
said can be used against him—anything from his mouth, and
anything from anybody else's mouth.

When the police are reaching out to the family, they are not
contacting you out of the blue. There's a reason for it. Be extremely aware of what you say, *at all times*. It is absolutely essential that
the *entire* family understands how to respond in these situations.

❑ **Social media sites like Facebook and Twitter now play a**
huge role in prosecutions. Detectives are constantly going on
these sites to look at the accounts of young people charged with
crimes to see what their social media affiliations are and to monitor the exchanges among suspects and their friends and family
members. They're looking for gang affiliations, symbols, and mottoes that might link a young person to other criminal types—
even something as simple or seemingly harmless as clicking "like"

on a page or a post considered suspicious. Everything you do on the Internet is subject to somebody being able to trace it and possibly use it against you.

❏ **Live your life as if there are eyes on you at all times.** Because you never know.

CHAPTER 9: THE PRISON-INDUSTRIAL COMPLEX

The Vicious Cycle

❏ **To a remarkable degree, imprisoning black males in the** United States has become a big business, resulting in the creation of hundreds of thousands of jobs across the nation and billions in profits for major corporations. The total US corrections market is worth an estimated $70 billion.

❏ **After the implementation of the War on Drugs, with its** mandatory sentencing guidelines and dramatically expanded focus on incarceration, the US penal population exploded from around 300,000 to more than 2 million, with drug convictions accounting for the majority of the increase. The US is the world's most prolific jailer, with rates of incarceration that dwarf every developed country in the world, including Russia, China, and Iran.

❏ **New York City, Arizona, Atlanta, Alabama, Washington** state, Texas, Michigan, Pennsylvania, Los Angeles—across the nation, stories abound of police departments imposing arrest and ticket quotas on their officers to keep a steady stream of bodies flowing into the system and income flowing into city and state coffers. This practice is illegal in many states. It blatantly encourages police to find criminal behavior where there really isn't any, and to take the easiest shortcuts to find suspects. In most places, those shortcuts mean preying on black and His-panic youth—those whom mainstream society is most likely to believe are behaving criminally and for whom society is least likely to rise up in protest.

❑ **With the flow of prisoners receding because of the falling** crime rate, increasingly desperate officials have been turning to a new source for their inmates: Schools. The term "school-to-pris-on pipeline" is being used increasingly to describe systems where youngsters are criminalized and locked up for committing acts that in a previous era would barely get a rise out of the principal.

❑ **One of the most shocking ways law enforcement can keep** the revenue flowing is through asset forfeiture. When Congress passed the Comprehensive Crime Control Act in 1984 as part of the War on Drugs, it allowed law-enforcement agencies to pock-et the proceeds from forfeitures they were responsible for, which meant that local police who provided federal assistance on big drug cases were rewarded with a large percentage of the proceeds through a program called Equitable Sharing. The process soon ex-ploded, driven by this new profit motive. Proceeds raked in by the federal Justice Department went from $27 million in 1985 to $4.2 billion in 2012.

❑ **This system began to be used to seize cash and property** from regular citizens. Law enforcement officers just started tak-ing people's stuff, including people who hadn't been convicted or in many cases even accused of committing crimes. In some Texas counties, nearly 40 percent of police budgets come from forfeiture. Not surprisingly, most of the victims tended to be poor and black or Hispanic.

❑ **States have also taken to using the probation system as a** fund-raising mechanism. Money-starved towns across the country have hired for-profit businesses to collect cash from the citizenry for fines and fees accrued from the writing of tickets. When poor folks can't pay the hundreds and sometimes thousands of dollars in fees that can accumulate for something as simple as a parking or speeding ticket, they might find themselves sitting in a jail cell.

❏ **Most studies show that the number of people released** from prison who wind up returning within three years typically hovers around 40 percent. This tends to be a statement more about the scarce opportunities these former offenders find on the outside than their predilection for crime.

❏ **In addition to the difficulty of finding meaningful employ-**ment, former offenders have to contend with a long list of parole restrictions and requirements that make it inevitable that many of them will wind up back in a cell. In most states, nearly a third of those who return to prison are sent back because of "technical" violations, which means they have violated parole rules, rather than because they've committed another crime.

❏ **A staggering number of individuals and businesses are** profiting from the mass incarceration of African Americans. While each of us as individuals may not be in a position to fight the system, each of us *can* pressure our elected officials to dismantle these institutions and take the profit motive out of incarceration. That would be a huge step toward rescuing our communities and our young black males from the greedy jaws of this incredibly destructive system.

About the Authors

ROBBIN SHIP, ESQ., has almost two decades of experience as an attorney in the state of Georgia. She specializes in litigation with a concentration in criminal defense, primarily representing low- to moderate-income individuals. Shipp received her BA from Shaw University; her MPA from Georgia College and State University; and her JD from Walter F. George College of Law at Mercer University. She is a single parent to daughter Alexandria.

NICK CHILES received a share of the Pulitzer Prize for Spot News Reporting in 1992, and is also a two-time recipient of the National Education Reporting Award. Among his earlier books are the *New York Times* bestsellers *The Blueprint: A Plan for Living above Life's Storms* (co-written with Kirk Franklin) and *The Rejected Stone: Al Sharpton and the Path to American Leadership* (co-written with Sharpton). Chiles has also written six books with his wife, Denene Millner. A graduate of Yale University, Chiles lives in Atlanta with his wife and their two daughters, and his son is a student at Lafayette College.

Index